Love and Grace

GOD IN STEREO

Love and Grace

GOD IN STEREO

JAKE STRINGER

Copyright © 2015 by Jake Stringer

All rights reserved. No part of this book may be reproduced or transmitted in any form or by any means without the written permission of the Publisher.

ISBN: 978-0-692-48743-3

"This book is dedicated to my precious wife Michelle, who saw things in me long before I saw them in myself, who has birthed unto me my two beautiful children Harmon August and Journey James, and to this day is my best friend and lover, and biggest inspiration and supporter."

01
RECKLESS LOVE

1 John 4:10 - *Herein is love, not that we loved God, but that he loved us, and sent his Son to be the atoning sacrifice for our sins.*

I REMEMBER THE MARCH morning when my wife Michelle woke me at 4 A.M. As my brain slowly came out of sleep mode, and my vision cleared, I saw my wife's face inches from mine, and felt her hand on my back. She had a huge smile on her face. "What's going on babe?" I mumbled. She said nothing, just held up a positive pregnancy test. "We're pregnant!" she said beaming.

We would go on to scream, shout, and jump up and down later that morning, but in this moment we simply embraced and cried tears of joy together. We were so excited! My heart immediately began to swell with thoughts of how much I loved this offspring of mine. I was pleased with this baby already, and *he* (as we found out later) wasn't even born yet. I began to hope for him to understand that my love for him was without condition, and beyond measure. I was already proud of him. I had always dreamed of a son, but in that particular instant, when it became a reality that I was actually going to have one, a burning, passionate desire for a close relationship with him, and for him to NEVER question my love for him, overwhelmed my heart! Wow! Remembering that moment brings tears to my eyes right now! I love him SO MUCH, and my heart continually expands to house more love for him by the second!

But, do you realize Harmon had never done anything for me? He had never worked for me. He had never followed any house rules to earn approval from me. He had never built a temple for me. He had never made any sacrifices to me. He had never gone to seminary for me. He had never performed a single task, yet I loved him, approved of him, and was infinitely and immovably pleased with him! While he was only a thought, long before Michelle was even pregnant, I loved him free from what he could DO for me. In fact, my son's performance for me, NEVER EVEN ENTERED MY THOUGHT PROCESS ABOUT HIM. After all, He is my son, not my servant.

> **John 15:15** – *"No longer do I call you servants, for a servant does not know what his master is doing; but I have called you friends, for all things that I heard from My Father I have made known to you."*

Take a moment and think of how you love a child you have now, or how you plan on loving your unborn children. Do you currently, or would you ever say to yourself, "If my child would just perform for me I could love them, but if they don't, I will withhold my love. I thoroughly enjoy my child's perception that my love for them is a vicious, hurtful cycle where my love and approval is being perpetually given and taken away from them based on their performance. I take great pleasure watching my child struggle and desperately try to earn and maintain my approval. I like to kick back with a bucket of popcorn and a Coke to observe my child on the never-ending hamster wheel of maintaining my approval and love."

I pray you don't view your children like that! Lucky for you, I choose to give you the benefit of the doubt, and assume you do not love your children this way! Why not though? Why is it that you would never want your precious child to ever question your love? I submit that it is because you are made in the image of God. You are divinely designed to love unconditionally as He does.

You see, when the atmosphere between a parent and child is one of performance, the parent is perceived as a slave master, not a loving parent. Instead of the relationship's foundation being love that is extended for free from the parent to the child, the foundation is love that is earned by the child performing well in the parent's eyes. Because of this, as time passes the parent begins to realize they have no voice into the child's life. Even if the parent has a loving word for the child one day the child does not have ears to ear, because a performance atmosphere drowns out the voice of love. This is why most Christians struggle to hear the voice of God.

We need a revelation of God's perfect love for us apart from our performance, because that is what casts out the unhealthy fear that we are always disappointing God. If you can renew your mind to God's unconditional love for you, you can purge your performance mindset and begin to hear God clearly… He has been speaking beautiful, loving words over you all your life.

> **1 John 4:18** - *There is no fear in love. But perfect love drives out fear, because fear has to do with punishment. The one who fears is not made perfect in love.*

02
SONS NOT SLAVES

SO MANY OF us sit under teaching that paints us as rule-following slaves to religion, and God is our slave master, rather than teaching us the truth that we are unconditionally loved children of God, and He is our loving father who loves us apart from our performance. His love has to do with who He is, and who we are, not what we can do for Him.

This performance based teaching drowns out the voice of God's love in a believer's life, and the voice of love is the voice of God; God IS love. This teaching perpetuates fear, and fear has torment.

> **1 John 4:8 –** *Whoever does not love, does not know God, for GOD IS LOVE.*

1 John 4:18 – *There is no fear in love; but perfect love casteth out fear: because fear hath torment. He that feareth is not made perfect in love.*

What we need in order to clearly hear the voice of God, is a purging of the performance mindset, which unclogs our ears, and enables us to hear the good words God has been speaking over us all along.

This is just what the enemy wants: millions of Christians who are sons and daughters of God, who belong in the father's house, yet go through life ignorant of this reality. Many of us believe that we belong in the slave quarters at best. Because we are so performance minded, we measure our worthiness or unworthiness to dwell in the father's house by our latest good deed or evil deed. The God we perceive when we think like this is not our God at all. This performance mindset distorts our perception of Him to the point that our idea of God becomes a false idol that is actually nothing like Him. We conclude He is a harsh slave master… this is just what the enemy wants. Our God is not a demander; He is a supplier.

Nonetheless, this demented "deity" is the God so many Christians perceive. He is a God who extends and retracts his love yo-yo based on your religious performance. This God is a pervert. He is a false idol! He is a religious invention of man! Do we really believe we can teach this God, and expect people to continue calling Him holy and good?

And yet, many people continue to proclaim Christ despite being under this type of teaching. You may be one of these people: still proclaiming this God out of a sincere heart... or out of fear of Hell. If so, I passionately apologize to you on His behalf. You have been subjected to tragically incorrect teaching, and may be deeply hurt, but I praise God you have not turned from Him! However, in addition to people that are still proclaiming Christ, there are millions of God's precious children who have turned from Him, and decided He's not for them because of this type of wrong teaching.

> **Romans 2:4** - *Or do you despise the riches of His goodness, forbearance, and patience, not knowing that the goodness of God (not preaching hell) leads you to repentance?*

If you are either of these people, you must know that you have been taught lies! That is not God! That is not the good news! God's love for you burns insatiably and extravagantly inside His heart! So much so, that this love-fire couldn't be contained, and manifested physically in the person of Jesus Christ! The Cross is God's eternal declaration of His desperation for intimacy with you!

I declare God wants to heal your heart! He wants to liberate you through a life-changing revelation of His unconditional love for you in the mighty name of Jesus! It is my prayer, that through this book, you can step into the liberty of His love, and bask in His unwavering adoration for your beautiful self the rest of your days! *{Wow!}*

You see, God can only love one way: UNCONDITIONALLY. Contrary to much wrong teaching, it is actually outside of God's ability to love conditionally. To God, conditional love isn't love at all. To Him, conditional love is counterfeit, and unconditional love is authentic. If you were to present the concept of conditional love to God, He would patiently listen to you, and then give a thoughtful reply that would go something like this: "Well, what you're describing wouldn't be love at all. Love has nothing to do with fulfilling conditions to earn something. That is called work."

Think of someone in your life who has always loved you no matter what. Someone you can always run boldly to no matter what you have done, or are doing, bad or good. This person always has time for you, and does not judge nor condemn you regardless of what you tell them. Doesn't their love just feel like a warm blanket? Their listening ear a safe place?

You are experiencing authentic, unconditional love. Your heart is receiving the fuel it was designed to run on from the very beginning: unconditional love and acceptance. So many Christians and non-Christians alike are running on love fumes… desperate for the heart fuel of unconditional love, and they don't even know it! This is not God's will. His will is for you to be firmly rooted in His unconditional love and acceptance, and for your tank to be filled continually to overflow.

You see, almost every area of our lives is performance based. Our promotions at work, raises, commissions, and rewards we give for our children's grades, etc., are all based on performance. Our brains are programmed to think in terms of performance. When someone loves us apart from our performance, simply because they value us, when we don't have to earn it, when we don't deserve it, when they love us FOR FREE, it short-circuits our brain.

The most difficult hurdle in receiving the love of God is realizing it is a FREE GIFT. You DO NOT have to earn it! It is not performance based! You are not undeserving, nor deserving of God's love based on your performance. God's love for you is 0% related to your performance! God's love is like oxygen; it is simply present for you to breathe in and out. Like oxygen you are surrounded by it at all times. You are enveloped by it. It sustains you. You don't have to earn oxygen; it is there for you to partake of without you having to perform for it. Oxygen is a free gift from God, just like His love.

God's love is not merited through good behavior, nor is it relinquished through poor behavior. The performance-based systems of the world, and an overwhelmingly "performance teaching," religious church deafen us to the voice of unconditional love, which is what God is ACTUALLY saying. He is a loving whisper on repeat, saying, "I love you child. No matter what. All the time. I adore you. I value you. You are mine. You are precious. I can't live without you." It is so unlike the world system, we must renew our mind to it… we must learn to think differently, and that can take a little time.

Would you consider me a good father to Harmon if I held in my possession the measure of oxygen that he needed to survive; the oxygen that is essential for his life to be sustained and to function properly, and I only gave him short gasps of it based on what he did for me? Based on his performance? Am I a loving father if I say, "Harmon, if you tithe to me I will give you enough of this oxygen to get you through another day. Harmon, if you do these five things without making a single mistake I'll give you a taste?"

NO! You would call Child Protective Services on me, and I would rightly be imprisoned for child abuse! And yet, we portray God this way. We ask people to worship this God, and call Him holy and good? Huh? How can we ever trust, and boldly approach such a monster? Even if someone receives the Lord based on this presentation of Him, the very birthplace of his or her relationship with Him is not one of trust. From the beginning they are handicapped by a concept of Him that prevents trust and intimacy, and perpetuates the fear of disappointment, and the expectation of punishment.

It is time to acquit God. I effortlessly loved my son apart from his performance before he was even conceived. How much more now that he is here in the flesh, and I can get to know him through our close relationship! As his performance for me never entered my thoughts about him, our performance never enters God's mind as a determining factor for His love either. He is not a monster. He does not have a performance-based thought pattern like the world does.

However, the church rarely represents Him this way. Rather, He is portrayed to the world as an angry, demanding, nearly impossible to appease, UNloving, disaster causing, sinner killing, genocidal, insecure megalomaniac. We scare people into "obedience," with turn or burn sermons displaying the fiery indignation of an angry God. Sound familiar?

I am here to tell you that God can only love you

unconditionally. He is bound to unconditional love. To believe, "My God loves me conditionally," is an idolatrous statement; for you are not describing the God of the Bible… you are describing some other false God. This is where most Christians are… "God loves me IF." In their mind, their standing before God is directly related to their recent behavior or performance for Him. The essential point to notice however is that although in their mind their standing before God may be performance based, IN HIS MIND THAT IS NOT TRUE AT ALL. Your standing before God IN HIS MIND is not based on YOUR performance at all. So, let us learn how He views us in His mind, and then agree with what He says.

You see we've always understood confession through the lens of sin consciousness, in other words being mindful of our sin. In fact, most concepts we have in Christianity we stain with sin consciousness. For example, we assume confession means to tell God how disgusting, sinful, and worm-like we are, and this somehow pleases Him and makes us spiritual and humble. This type of thinking is rampant in the body of Christ. It sounds like this: "Oh God, have mercy on your worm servant! Please tolerate me for one more day! Have mercy on my disgusting, repelling self!" This outlook is completely backwards. Have we learned nothing from Christ's redemptive work on the Cross? The Cross is proof of our worthiness and beauty to God. In fact, we are so worthy and beautiful to Him that He wants to enter into a MARRIAGE RELATIONSHIP with each and every one of us. That certainly says something about God and His love, but it also says something about us! It says that we are lovely! For example, my wife marrying me says something about her... primarily that she's merciful, LOL! Thank you Jesus! But, in all seriousness, her marrying me says something about me too! It says that I'm lovely to her! <u>Christ is proof you are lovely to God!</u> The fact that He wants to enter into a marriage relationship with you is proof of your loveliness. How much more proof do you need that you are lovely to God?!

The truth is, <u>confession means, "to agree with</u>." If we can understand this word without factoring sin consciousness into the equation, we can experience mind renewal. You see God says that He loves you apart from your performance, so true "confession" would be to agree with Him, and speak forth something like this, "God, thank you that your love for me is unconditional, and based on who You are as a loving Father, and who I am as your lovely child. Your love for me is not based on the things I can do for you. Thank you for your unconditional love Father!" When you begin saying things like that, you are entering into true confession. You are agreeing with God.

When you continue to think like a slave, speaking forth your unworthiness and despicability, you are not actually confessing the Word of God; you are disagreeing with it. It is prideful and arrogant to disagree with God. If you want to be spiritual and humble, agree with Him, and confess your son-ship and righteousness, and His unconditional love for you! Sin consciousness, which is perpetuated by legalistic thinking, causes you to think contrary to your design. That is why we can never find happiness in legalism and religion. Let us learn to exit the legalistic mind, and think and believe like we are designed to: as sons and daughters, and we shall begin to experience abundant life.

With that in mind, let's take stock together of what you are believing. If you would, ask yourself a few questions:

1. Do I believe it's possible for God's love for me to ever waver?
2. In my mind, do I ever assume God's love for me is withdrawn based on my performance or behavior?
3. Do I ever believe I've lost my salvation or righteousness (right standing) before God because of what I've done, or certain sins I've committed?
4. Do I believe after losing my salvation because of an evil deed, I then regain my salvation by performing good deeds, or carrying out specific religious duties for a man-appointed, arbitrary amount of time?
5. Do I believe God's love is initially extended to me as a gift, but the burden of convincing God to continue loving me is on my shoulders? … that I must maintain and sustain His love for me through my performance, by my own strength and willpower?
6. Do I believe God is displeased with me at any point?

If you answered with an emphatic "NO!" to all of these questions, CONGRATULATIONS! You are firmly rooted in the unconditional love of your Father God! If you answered yes to any, there is room for you to grow in the knowledge of the unconditional love of God! Either way, I invite you to embark on this journey with me to learn more about how no matter what you have done, God loves you unconditionally, immovably, enthusiastically, joyfully, insatiably, extravagantly, and comprehensibly!

03
WHERE DID I PUT MY PHONE?!

AGAPĒ/AGAPAŌ– GOD'S KIND of love, a parental, mature, sacrificial kind of love, "to take pleasure in the thing, prize it above all other things, be unwilling to abandon it or do without it." To be fond of, to love dearly, to welcome, to be well pleased, and to be content with. It is concerned that the loved one is always provided for, usually at cost to the bearer. A love-feast. Agape puts the beloved first and sacrifices pride, self-interest and possessions for the sake of that beloved. This is the love that God has for us, which inspired him to sacrifice His son, and for His son to obey and sacrifice himself. It is a love of supreme greatness.

Before we go further, I want to personalize this definition. This may stretch you, and you may think, "this is too radical for me." This may push your religious buttons and make you angry. Nevertheless, this truth remains: that for you to progress with God, for you to begin walking in peace and joy, it is vital that you settle in your heart just how radically and unconditionally God loves you despite what religion has always taught you. You are worthy to be intimate with God. The Cross shouts that! Allow yourself to soak in His love for YOU, and give Him the chance to persuade your heart of your incalculable value and preciousness to Him! I encourage you to say this definition out loud repeatedly, and allow the Holy Spirit to begin to minister to you, and show you just how loved you are. I want you to say it out loud because faith comes by hearing.

> **Romans 10:17** – *"Faith (persuasion of the heart) comes by hearing, and hearing by the Word of God."*

Let's declare together: " Father, you radically, recklessly, and extravagantly love me! You take pleasure in me, You prize me above all other things, and You are unwilling to abandon me or do without me. You are fond of me. You love me dearly. You welcome me. You are well pleased with me. You are content with me. You are concerned that I am always provided for, at cost to You. You put me first. You have such an abundance of extravagant love for me; I can fearlessly feast on it anytime. Thank you father that you love me so extravagantly and recklessly!!

God, I thank you, that whenever I feel under attack, under condemnation, or am questioning your love, that the Holy Spirit will bring these truths immediately to my remembrance and flood my heart with peace and rest. Amen!"

You see, we must have an accurate understanding of the actual definition of the love of God, because general knowledge of the definitions of words changes over time. This does not mean the definition actually changed, only the way the majority of people understand a word upon hearing it. Without even trying, when you hear the phrase, "God loves you," you filter it through your personal definition of the word love based on culture, and life experience.

Even if God's idea of His love for you is different than yours, once it's filtered through your definition of love, what is yielded will become your personal reality. This will remain the case until you are made aware that another definition exists, and you make yourself available to have your definition redefined. It is my prayer that you allow yourself to have your understanding of God' s love renewed, redefined, and realigned to the truth. To illustrate this concept, let's take a word like "gay." These days, the definition of the word is far different than it was say in 1930. The word once simply meant "happy."

Let's say I lived in the 1930's, and after high school my best friend Jimmy moves away for college. Facebook and cell phones do not exist yet, so we continue to stay in touch through letters after he's moved away. We begin to write each other reminiscing about all the good times we had growing up. Throughout the letters phrases appear like: "do you remember how gay we were that one night?" "We used to be so gay when we were together." "I just haven't met anybody else that I can be as gay with as I was with you." At the time I am writing these letters, I mean nothing about homosexuality. I am simply referring to how much fun we used to have.

Now, fast-forward 70 years. I have just passed away. My family then begins to sort through my estate. My granddaughter stumbles upon a beautiful wooden box in the attic, and opens it to discover a collection of letters. Gripped by curiosity, she begins to read.

"Oh my God!" she screams in shock. The phrases are highlighted to her as if only they are backlit. "None of our friends were as gay as we were." "Ever since you moved, I haven't found another friend that I can be gay with."

"Mom!" she yells. "You've got to come up here!" "Prepare yourself, I think Grandpa was secretly gay!" They continue to sift through these letters only to find more confirmation. Scandal begins to spread like wildfire among my family and friends. My precious widow is devastated to discover that although I was married to her for sixty years, and we had four beautiful children together, all that time I was only pretending to be in love with her; I really wanted to be with a man. She believed I loved only her, that we were soul mates. Heartbroken, she feels cheap, deceived, and betrayed.

However, all of this heartbreak is based on a miscommunication! All this destruction is because they are concluding I was gay according to the current, cultural definition of gay, not the definition of gay I understood when I wrote the letters! It is creating a huge mess, and causing heartache, and it's not even true… I only meant I never found a friend with whom I could have as good of a time as I could with my friend Jimmy!

The same concept is true with the Word of God.

Because of a lack of the knowledge of what words mean in the original languages of the bible, what the writers meant when they wrote those words, and the assumption that the words mean what we think they mean now; we are missing out on the fullness of what God wants us to know about His love for us and SO MANY OTHER TOPICS. The more we dig into the original language, the more GOOD NEWS we find!!

For example, let's take one aspect of the word "agapē," which is defined at the beginning of this chapter. Let's use the aspects of the definition that say, "to be well pleased with, to be content with." Now, let's read the most famous verse in the bible using just that one aspect of the definition of God's love, and see how the depth and power in that verse comes alive.

> **John 3:16 –** *"For God so loved the world, that he gave his only begotten Son, that whosoever believeth in him should not perish, but have everlasting life." "For God was so well pleased with, and content with the world, that he gave his only begotten Son, that whosoever believeth in him should not perish, but have everlasting life."*

"But I thought God was displeased and discontent with man because of man's disobedience, and needed to take out this utter disdain and discontentment on Jesus, so that He could tolerate us again." I declare the bible does not teach that. Religion has taught that. The Bible teaches

that God sent divinity itself in the bodily form of Jesus Christ to reconcile us, to convince us that we ARE valued, He IS well pleased with us, and that He WAS content with man, in the midst of man's disobedience. God has always been convinced of our value; we are the ones that need convincing.

In fact, you are so valuable, and worth such a high price, God could not even redeem you by sending an Angel, for you are a being of too high an order. He had to send Himself inside of Himself, flowing through the veins of Himself. You are that valuable. Somebody say amen! Oh, praise the Lord! JOY JOY JOY!!

But, we'll never know the power of what God means when He says He loves us unless we educate ourselves on the ACTUAL definition of the word, on what He means when He says it, and allow ourselves to see past our narrow, cultural understanding of love.

You MUST renew your mind to what God means when He says He loves you, for it will revolutionize your life, and release the abundant life and freedom God always intended for you to walk in. Abundant life manifests through your understanding!

Think of something with which you are immensely pleased and content. Let's say it's your cell phone. What happens when you lose your cell phone? Does its value decrease when it's lost? Does its location make you any less pleased or content with it? Why do you turn your house upside down frantically searching for it? If anything, when you lose that phone, its value seems to increase, right?

Now, think of something you're not particularly pleased or content with. When you lose it, you just let it go because it's not of any particular value to you, right? You think, "Well, I can do without that thing," because you're not particularly pleased or content with it. It holds no particular value to you.

Let us then ask ourselves what God did when man became lost. Did God just let us go? No, God did everything he could to redeem man when man became lost, because He WAS content with man, and He WAS pleased with man. He sent divinity itself inside of a man to restore a broken relationship with mankind because He WAS content with man. Man is God's masterpiece. When a painter paints their masterpiece, they do not discard it, they treasure it!

God would not have sent Jesus to redeem you, if He was not pleased and content with you. God would not have sent Jesus if you were not of immense value to Him! He would've just thought, *"Well, I'm not particularly content with them, so I'll just let them go."* Man's value did not change simply because he was lost. If anything, in God's heart and mind, man's value increased! There was intense passion and urgency in the heart of God to heal and restore man's condition. Being lost does not bring forth a loss of value.

You see, if you are not rooted in the actual definition of God's love for you, you won't know just how pleased and content with you He is. God's unconditional love for you is a pre-existing truth in which you can have faith, not something you earn from Him by performing. There is no, "God loves me IF." There is only, "God loves me unconditionally already, let me believe this truth that already exists and have life!"

If you're not aware of what God means when He declares He loves you, you can begin to believe that God loves you just like your earthly father who was perpetually discontent with you, just like your spouse who hit or verbally abused you, just like your spouse who left you, or just like your friend who betrayed you. You may begin thinking of our cultural definition of love, or your mistakes in life, of people you've hurt, people who've disappointed you when you thought they loved you, of the way your mother loved you, or like in my case, the way my father didn't love me.

Footnote: *The above is a combination of the Strong's concordance, and Thayer's Greek Lexicon definitions of the Greek words "agapē (uh-gaw-pay)," and "agapaō," which are the Greek words used in the New Testament to describe the love of God.*

04
BELIEF BENEFIT PACKAGE

WE MUST UNDERSTAND that what we believe has the power to dramatically alter our quality of life, regardless of whether what we are believing is true or not. You see, God created us as creatures at the mercy of what we believe. What do I mean? Well, the things we believe will lead to actions based on those beliefs, and subsequently those actions lead to the consequences resulting from those actions, whether good or bad. What we believe is the root, and the actions that follow our beliefs are the fruit. If you want different fruit, you must dig up the existing root, and replace it with a different seed and allow the new seed to take root and bring forth different fruit. You cannot simply cut the fruit and let the root remain.

Take Adam for example. Through the deception of the enemy, Adam's belief was changed. He went from believing with childlike innocence that God already made him complete and lacking nothing, to believing God had kept things from him, and he was incomplete. This new belief about himself led Adam to eat from the tree to try and gain something, when God had already given him everything. Do you see what happened? Adam's belief changed, which led to his actions changing. His belief preceded his actions.

We see this concept in our every day lives as well; the concept that we act on what we believe. I remember when I was eighteen and a freshman at the University of Kentucky... I was a good tennis player in High School, and had been offered a few partial tennis scholarships to some really good Division II schools, but I was in love, and wanted to be where my girlfriend Jenn was. Naturally I chose to go to the University of Kentucky where she was going. I was convinced Jenn and I were meant to be, and we without a doubt would be spending the rest of our lives together. No one could convince me otherwise. When anyone tried to suggest a different direction for me, I did not have "ears to hear." I was going where she was.

Well, about a month into our freshman year, Jenn calls me to her dorm because she has something to tell me. She begins sharing this story of a party she was at the previous night with some of the other girls from her floor. She began to share about how she was just sitting by herself, and a guy came up and began to ask her how she was, and they started talking. She didn't think anything of it, only that he was a really nice guy who seemed genuinely concerned. Well, she says that they talked for hours, and he begins to tell her how amazing she is, how excited he is to have met her, and things like that.

She tells me she doesn't know why, or how it even

happened, but they started kissing, and kept kissing. My heart was beating fast, and I was feeling panicked and frantic inside. *"Is this really happening?" I thought. "The girl that I thought I was going to marry, is telling me how she cheated me on last night?" My mind was racing. "Only a month into school? Is she just like all these other college chicks? Is she not different like I thought she was? This is crap. I could be playing tennis somewhere right now; instead I'm here listening to this garbage! You mean she just wants to party and experiment like everyone else? She makes out with the first guy that says hello to her freshman year even though we are together?" I grew angrier and angrier… I asked her why at least fifteen times… "why? why would you do this?!"*

You see, this was especially devastating because only a couple of months before, we had an instance where a guy from school started a rumor that he had made out with Jenn while we were together, and it was a guy that I knew was totally into her. Because of this I didn't believe her denial at first. Because I was so insecure and jealous all the time, it took her weeks to convince me that it never happened. Looking back, I was so insecure, jealous, and controlling that I honestly want to puke when I think about it! We were passed that incident though, and I thought we were stronger for it. So for her to tell me this, after what had just happened that summer was so hard.

She apologized over and over and over. We were both crying uncontrollably. I was sitting on her roommate's bed and she on hers… I couldn't bring myself to even sit by her I was so angry. After a few hours of talking, I finally calmed down enough to where I could think relatively clearly.

I was exhausted. We had been crying and yelling for hours. As I began to put my shoes back on to leave, I said to her, "Jenn, this is it. I can't be with you anymore. I am too hurt by what you did. I thought you were different. If you were entertaining the thought of making out with other people, I don't understand why you wouldn't break up with me first, and then go make out with someone." I wanted to hurt her heart like she'd hurt mine. I was unnecessarily mean to her as I told her we needed to break up because she had hurt me so badly. <u>Hurt people hurt people</u>, amen? Amen. I told her that there was nothing special about her, and that I hoped she enjoyed the rest of her life alone. I was speaking from a place of hurt. I told her all the standards like, "Good luck finding another guy as good as me." HAHAHA It was very dramatic.

Amazingly, life did somehow go on after this happened. I made some great friends in the engineering dorm across from mine, and we had a really fun year. About halfway into sophomore year though, I was hanging out at my house with my friends Rob and Patrick from my band Corona Drive (the name of the street we grew up on, creative huh?!). We kept all the music equipment where I lived, so we usually hung out at my place.

We were having a great time, (illegally) drinking a few beers, and we started talking about Jenn. I hadn't really hung out with Jenn, or our high school friends for a while because of what happened, but Rob and Patrick had. As we began talking about her, my mind instantly went back to our final night together in her dorm… the night she told me she cheated. My countenance dropped, and I just looked down at the ground and started talking about how

I still couldn't believe how things ended with her. How it was so hard for me to believe she cheated like that. She was such a sweet girl. I lifted my eyes to see if Rob or Patrick had anything to say, and noticed they were giving each other a funny look. "What is it?" I asked. "Why are you guys looking at each other like that?"

Rob says to Patrick, "We should tell him man."

"I don't know dude, we told Jenn we wouldn't," Patrick replied.

I was like, "Tell me what?" "What's going on?"

"Jake man," Rob began. "Jenn never cheated on you."

"Huh? What?" I replied. "What do you mean?"

"Dude, she made that whole story up because she didn't have the guts to break up with you. She knew if she told you she cheated on you, you would break up with her."

"You've got to be kidding man!" I yelled. "How do you know that?"

"She told us man, and made us swear we'd never tell you, but I just don't feel right about it. I feel like you need to know. I can't keep it from you any longer." I started laughing initially. The first thing I felt was relief, followed by amazement.

Then my mind began to wonder, "Hold on... You mean that whole story was made up? All the details were fabricated? All the tears she cried were an act?" I started to get angry again!

Eventually, I learned a lot from this experience. I learned a great deal about how insecurity, jealousy, and control have no place in a relationship. They are poisonous, and they drive people away. This is why God pursues us in such a gentlemanly fashion without ever forcing our hand. I was so insecure, jealous, and controlling, that she didn't think I was reasonable enough to just break up with the old fashion way. Her perception of me broke my heart. I didn't even realize how I appeared to her. I understood the effect my jealousy and insecurity had on her, and it changed me forever.

The reason I share this story, is to illustrate that what Jenn actually set out to do to me was very similar to what the serpent set out to do to Adam: it was to change what I believed about her, thus leading me to change my actions. She wanted to change my belief from, *"Jenn is the girl I want to be with for the rest of my life,"* which is the belief that caused me to want to be WITH her, to *"Jenn is absolutely not the type of girl I want to be with at all. I need to break up with her."*

She knew that if she could change my belief about her, she would change my actions. She knew that instead of wanting to stay with her, I would want to break up with her. Even though what she got me to believe about her WAS A TOTAL LIE, I STILL BELIEVED IT, and I acted upon my new belief. I broke up with her according to her plan, based on the lie that I believed.

05
FLUSHING OUT THE TOXINS

THANKFULLY, THIS FALLACY that I believed about her was exposed as a lie, and I was able to remove it from my belief system. The scary part was that I believed a lie and did not even know it! You see, Rob's conscience was tearing him up as he sat in the room with me, armed with this knowledge that what I believed about Jenn was a lie. As someone who cared for me, he understood that although there might be initial shock on my part when I heard the truth about Jenn; it was to my benefit to know the truth.

In the very same way, my conscience will not allow me to keep the truth of God's unconditional love and Grace towards you a secret from you, nor from the rest of the world!! I have benefitted in indescribable ways from receiving a revelation of Grace, God's unconditional love, and the value of man apart from his sin, and I know it will benefit you to know these truths as it has me! These revelations are the essential building blocks of the victorious christian walk! They will keep you full of life and peace! As opposed to religion, which keeps us running on empty.

One of the primary goals of this book is to expose the lies of the enemy, and lies you've learned in religion that you may believe, so that you can remove them from your belief system and dramatically improve your quality of life. Because, if you don't believe those lies anymore, you won't act on them, and therefore won't have to endure the negative consequences of the actions that follow those beliefs! Praise God!

In the very same way that Jenn convinced me to believe a lie and therefore changed my actions, the enemy convinced Adam to believe a lie, knowing that changing Adam's belief would change his actions, and lead to negative consequences Adam could not reverse. Even though it was a lie, Adam believed it. This led to him acting upon the lie he believed… Again… EVEN THOUGH IT WAS A LIE. Adam believed the serpent's story that God withheld from Him, and that only if He ate from the tree of the knowledge of good and evil could Adam gain what God withheld (not true), so He ate from the tree of the knowledge of good and evil to try and become what he already was. His change of belief led to a change in action, which led to negative consequences. Because he believed the serpent's lie that he was _incomplete_, and missing something, this belief led to the action of eating from the tree to try and gain what would make him _complete_. But, the train didn't stop there though.

In the first instance with the tree, Adam's belief was

altered by a deception from the enemy. However, following the serpent's deception, Adam's beliefs were subsequently attacked by his OWN guilty conscience. Satan could now take a break, sit back, have a beer, and laugh as Adam's guilty conscience began to devour him. Satan simply pushed over the first domino. Satan caused Adam to begin reasoning from a guilty conscience, instead of an innocent conscience. All of Adam's thoughts originated from the place of, "I have disappointed God, what can I do to regain His approval," rather than, "I am God's son in whom He is well pleased apart from what I've done."

06
IN YOUR MIND OR GOD'S?

PREPARE FOR A radical truth: Adam had not disappointed God! He ASSUMED He had, based on his sinful action, but he had not! It was only a belief in Adam's mind, not God's!

Where was Adam alienated? Where was Adam an enemy of God's? Was it in God's mind? NO!! It was in Adam's MIND. NOT GOD'S MIND, and NOT IN REALITY. This is the false reality the enemy created in Adam's mind by deceiving him into believing lies about God and himself, and it's the same one he tries to create in our minds. His strategy is unchanged.

Don't just take my opinion on this. Allow the word of God to wash your poisonous guilty conscience in the innocence of Jesus Christ!

Colossians 1:21 – *"And you, that were sometime alienated and enemies in YOUR mind by wicked* *works, yet now hath he reconciled In the body of his flesh through death, to present you holy and unblameable and unreproveable in his sight"*

I want you to realize something that will change your life. You ARE NOT alienated from God, nor are you an enemy of God's in GOD'S MIND, and what is true in His mind is the ONLY TRUE REALITY. In Him you live, and move, and have your being, He is near, and He will never leave you nor forsake you (Acts 17:28, Deut. 31:6).

You, like me, probably have not lived a life that is perfect in deed. Like me, you have most likely made some mistakes. What happens, is that like Adam we assume that we are alienated from God, that we are His enemies, and that we are disappointing to Him because of our "evil deeds." Because we remain more conscious of our sin than we are conscious of our Savior Jesus Christ, and how He has in fact cleansed us of ALL SIN, we begin to agree with the serpent, rather than agreeing with God.

Your quality of life will only begin to improve as you agree with what is true in the mind of God. If you stubbornly continue to agree with the serpent, you will continue to be condemned and alienated from the life of God. God is not inflicting this alienation. You are not alienated in His mind. In YOUR MIND you're alienating yourself by being sin conscious, instead of conscious of the cleansing blood of Jesus Christ.

God's will is for you NOT TO BE SIN CONSCIOUS ANYMORE! He wants you to be JESUS CONSCIOUS. But, you must agree with God that you've been cleansed for deliverance to manifest! I declare to you, Jesus has fully cleansed you, and you are not alienated in God's mind! Maybe you have felt alienated simply because you were not made aware of the truth… if that's the case, now you know the truth! You are reconciled, blameless, holy, and unreproveable in His sight!

Despite the truth that you are not alienated in God's mind, you do still have the power to SELF-banish from the life of God… and this happens IN YOUR MIND through your sin-conscious evaluation of yourself. God has given you your own mind and thoughts with which to do as you please. You will always conclude you are alienated if you continue to judge yourself by your evil deeds, but God is not doing that. Why do you keep doing it? This is never happening in God's mind… it's only happening in your mind.

The second half of the verse declares your reality in God's mind, which is the ONLY TRUE REALITY. Let me summarize: "You who feel alienated in YOUR mind, listen up… the truth is that you have been irreversibly reconciled (brought back into close relationship, the OPPOSITE of being alienated) through what Jesus has done! He presents you holy, unblameable, and unreproveable in God's sight! Agree with God!" If you choose to reason from any reality that is not that reality in God's mind, you are reasoning from a false reality, and you are limiting your own potential quality of life. By agreeing with the serpent, you are preventing abundant life from manifesting for you.

The sin conscious mind is a mind that is agreeing with satan. You are agreeing with his false accusation that you are alienated from God because of your mistakes, just like

Adam did. I challenge you to AGREE WITH WHAT IS TRUE IN GOD'S MIND, not with the accusation of the serpent. It is more humble to agree with God that you have been cleansed, than to keep exalting your mistakes above the all powerful, cleansing blood of Jesus Christ.

It is actually prideful, and self-righteous, to choose to continue to judge yourself based on your evil deeds. You are arrogantly disagreeing with God, who believes that Jesus has completely cleansed you. Humility is to agree with God, and God says, "Child, have peace, for the blood of Jesus Christ has cleansed you and you are not alienated, you are brought near, all the time, let us fellowship together as father and son/daughter and enjoy each other without sin being part of our discussion. Will you agree with me child? Will you allow me to love you without taking your performance into account?"

07
BATHE YOUR CONSCIENCE IN THE INNOCENT BLOOD OF THE LAMB

THE WORLD IS so performance based… we are so accustomed to being punished and rewarded based on our performance, that we insert that viewpoint into the way we relate to God. We must renew our mind to the truth that we don't relate to God based on our performance, we relate to Him based on the reality that He is our loving Father, and we are his beloved child, and this reality does not change based on our behavior. We have the same reality before God that Jesus has because of His work on the Cross. Your sin debt is paid in full, and your righteousness account is overflowing! Your sin balance is zero before God! You can stop being sin debt conscious once and for all, right now! Thank you Jesus!

Here are some scriptures that should make it

abundantly clear to you that God's will is for you to have no more consciousness of sin, and that you have in fact been cleansed of all sin by the blood of Jesus Christ! You have no more sin debt! Your debt has been paid past, present, and future.

> **Hebrews 9:14** - *How much more shall the blood of Christ, who through the eternal Spirit offered himself without spot to God, purge your conscience from dead works to serve the living God?*
>
> **Hebrews 10:1-2** - *For the law, having a shadow of the good things to come, and not the very image of the things, can never with these same sacrifices, which they offer continually year by year, make those who approach perfect.* **2** *For then would they not have ceased to be offered? For the worshipers, once purified, would have had no more consciousness of sins.*
>
> **Hebrews 10:12-14** – *But this man, after He had offered ONE SACRIFICE FOR SINS FOREVER, sat down at the right hand of God: from henceforth expecting until his enemies be made his footstool. For BY ONE OFFERING He HAS PERFECTED FOREVER them that are sanctified.*
>
> **Ephesians 1:7** – *In whom we have redemption through his blood, the forgiveness of sins, according to the riches of His GRACE.*

Ephesians 4:32 – *And be kind to one another, tenderhearted, forgiving one another, even as God for Christ's sake has forgiven you.*

Colossians 2:13 – *And you, being dead in your sins and the uncircumcision of your flesh, has he quickened together with him, having forgiven ALL TRESPASSES.*

I Pet 2:24 – *Who his own self bare our sins in his own body on the tree, that we, being dead to sins, should live unto righteousness, by whose stripes we are healed.*

Part of living the Christian life that the church has been failing to teach people, is that we are called to have no more consciousness of sins! One of the best parts of being saved is being free to stop thinking about sin all the time, and start thinking about what Jesus has done for you all the time! This will deliver you from the prisons of self-consciousness and self-focus, and birth sin-destroying thankfulness for Jesus and His Grace in your heart.

The enemy does not want you to have this revelation though, because it will bring freedom to your life. He knows if you've already received Jesus, the best thing he can still do is deceive you into continuing to beat yourself up with sin consciousness, which will render you condemned, and totally consumed with monitoring your own religious behavior. Behave well, have peace, behave poorly, bye bye peace. If this is you… a born-again Christian who has still been living in condemnation, and sin consciousness, you can stop right now! Receive the truth, which is there is no more condemnation for you, and God's will is for you to have no more consciousness of sin! Your debt is fully paid, have peace.

> **Romans 8:1** – *"There is therefore now NO CONDEMNATION for those who are in Christ Jesus."*

You see, this is the Gospel! The TOO GOOD TO BE TRUE NEWS! Sin has been paid for, it is time to move on into a love relationship with your loving Heavenly Father that is in no way based on your performance, which is what He has desired from the VERY BEGINNING. However, the true Gospel of Grace has been buried under the dirt of legalism and religion for so long, that when it is unearthed, it is hard to recognize.

08
DEBT FREE

TO ILLUSTRATE, I want you to imagine you go to Best Buy and purchase a 70 inch TV on credit. Man, you are excited. You get it home, hook up your HD satellite TV, your Blu-ray player, your 7.1 surround sound home theater system, and you are in Heaven.

You faithfully make your first few payments, but then catastrophe strikes and you fall on hard times. Money is running short, so you begin to prioritize your bills, knowing there are not enough funds to cover them all. You think, "I need to pay my rent first to keep this roof over my head, then my food, then my utilities, phone, etc., and you eventually decide that the TV payment is the one that gets put to the side. For a few months this continues, and before you know it you are 3 months delinquent on your big screen payment.

What begins to happen in your mind? What are you thinking about all the time? What is stopping you from fully enjoying life moment to moment? Debt consciousness. You will be thinking about your debt all the time. You will become totally debt-conscious. Even as you write your rent check, instead of being thankful that the check will clear, and you can keep the roof over your head, you will actually be thinking about that big screen TV payment. No matter what you do, you cannot get this debt off of your mind.

Then, one day, you start getting phone calls from a strange 1-800 number. Your debt-consciousness immediately communicates to you that it is the debt collector. They are calling to collect the debt you owe. The number of calls you receive from this number increases to five or six a day, and each time you avoid it. You know for sure that they are furious, because you are only conscious of what you've done wrong. Finally, one day, after avoiding countless calls, and deleting numerous voicemails without listening to them, you conjure up the courage to call them back. You cannot take it anymore. You simply have to figure out how to relieve the burden of this debt.

Leading up to this dreaded phone call, you have no doubt created this scenario in your mind about how the conversation is going to go. You know for sure that it is going to be extremely stressful and difficult. You will be on the phone for hours. You will be begging for mercy. You will be pleading for them not to repossess the TV. After a brief hold, the customer service representative comes on the line. Before they can finish saying hello, you desperately fumble into your story.

You spend the next fifteen minutes explaining your situation, and all the reasons you had to stop making the payment… you plead for mercy. You finally come to some sort of ending point and you ask, "Is there anything we can do? Is there some sort of alternative payment plan I can get on to begin to catch up? I cannot stand having this debt on my mind all the time anymore!"

The representative answers, "Sir, I am so sorry about what has been happening in your life, that is unfortunate, and I feel for you. However, I have been calling you six times a day, and have left you double-digit voicemails already. Have you not listened to any of them?"

"Well, no." You reply. "I didn't listen because I knew you would just be calling to hound me about my debt. I didn't have the courage to listen and be reminded of my debt, so I deleted them without listening."

"Well," the representative begins, "If you had just picked up the phone once, or had listened to only one of the many messages I have left you, you would know that I was only calling to inform you that your entire balance has been paid. Someone called in and knew you by name, and said they wanted to pay your TV off. You have a zero balance; you are paid in full. We just wanted to say thank you for financing the TV through us, and we needed to note in our computer system that we had spoken with you, and confirmed with you that your debt is paid before we could officially close your account."

Wow! That whole time you thought they were calling to collect a debt, but they were actually calling to inform you that your debt has been paid. They even left you voicemails telling you that you were debt free, but due to your fear and debt- consciousness you couldn't bring yourself to listen to the messages, as you thought it would just remind you of your debt. You avoided conversation with them because of your debt-consciousness. You could not fully enjoy life because of your debt- consciousness. You were bound in debt-consciousness, even though in reality you had been DEBT-FREE the entire time! You were experiencing an incredibly low quality of life because you believed the lie that you were indebted when you were not.

This is what has happened to the Gospel. People have been preaching a Gospel that is no Gospel at all. It is a message that makes God out to be the debt collector. Christians avoid conversations with God because they believe all He wants to do is remind them how they have come up short again this month, and He is angry. They believe God's mission is to remind them of their sin debt. They are experiencing a low quality of life due to this debt consciousness. This debt consciousness is satanic.

The reality is, God is like the bank handling your financing, and a preacher is supposed to be like the representative with whom you spoke. God keeps perfect books, and according to His records, you are SIN FREE! YOU HAVE NO SIN-DEBT! YOUR SIN-DEBT IS PAID! He now sends orders down from headquarters to the preacher to inform you that your debt has been paid!

09
AMBASSADORS GONE ROGUE

SO, A PASTOR is called to be a representative of this amazing news, trying to reach you to inform you that you are debt-free, not to remind you of a debt. A true minister of the Gospel is like that representative that was trying to reach you to inform you that your debt has been paid.

If you are a Pastor, ask yourself, "Have I been teaching my congregation that they have a sin-debt that needs paying? Am I their debt collector? Do I paint God out as a God that is using me to demand payment from them??" Or, "Am I exalting Jesus and his finished work on the Cross… and the sin payment He has made FOR ALL PEOPLE, rendering them debt-free, and telling them the amazing news that their debt has been paid?" If you have been using approach #1, you are a pastor who yourself has no understanding of the God you represent, and I say that in love. God loves you Pastor! And he wants to reveal the Gospel to you and turn your entire ministry around!

God is pursuing you with the true gospel… He is speaking to you, and leading you to YouTube videos, blogs, articles, this book possibly, to inform you of the truth, which is that YOUR DEBT HAS BEEN PAID! He doesn't want to remind you of your debt, He wants to declare to you that you are debt free! He sees you, his precious child, experiencing a quality of life far below the abundant one He planned for you because of your sin-consciousness. He wants to deliver you out of that bondage into the Promised Land!

This is the Gospel, the ministry of reconciliation, to which we are called. The bible refers us as ambassadors of the ministry of reconciliation. Sin no longer separates you, you have been reconciled, receive this truth and stop being conscious of a sin-debt that has been paid. Continuing to self-evaluate based on your sin is needless. Christ has paid it all! Have peace!

Religion puts you on a payment plan to pay your own sin-debt. Your religious behavior and good deeds are your monthly installments. If you don't do enough good deeds, debt-consciousness consumes you. Even the months you feel you've reached the imaginary amount of good deeds that it takes to reach high enough on Heaven's "good deed meter," and soothe your own debt conscience, it's only good for a month at best. You need a truth that can soothe your conscience from sin-debt for THE REST OF YOUR LIFE. This payment has been made, in the form of the precious blood of Jesus Christ. Somebody say Amen!

People avoid church for the same reason you were

avoiding the calls from the 1-800 number: they think the pastor just wants to remind them of their debt and sin. What a tragedy! This is completely unbiblical and contrary to the Gospel! A Pastor is supposed to exalt the payment that Jesus has already paid, and encourage people to receive this free gift, not condemn people and teach them that they're responsible to pay their own sin-debt.

You could never pay your own sin-debt. Christ was always destined to pay it for you… He is the lamb slain from before the foundation of the world. Your best day of religious good behavior is as filthy rags! Only the blood of Jesus Christ, shed on the Cross of Calvary, is powerful enough to pay that debt, and IT HAS! All you need to do is believe! Hear this message and simply respond with a "Praise God! Thank you, Jesus!" Have peace!

> **2 Cor 5:19-20** – *"To wit, that God was in Christ, RECONCILING THE WORLD UNTO HIMSELF, NOT IMPUTING THEIR SINS AGAINST THEM; and hath committed unto us the word of reconciliation. Now then we are ambassadors for Christ, as though God did beseech you by us: we pray you in Christ's stead, be ye reconciled to God."*

Notice, God declares us ambassadors of the message of reconciliation. This message declares that God has done His part to reconcile the entire world. His work is finished, all that's left is for people to believe and receive this free gift of righteousness!

The tragedy is that although this is the glorious gospel of Grace that the church has been entrusted with, it is not the message the church is known for preaching. Religion has gone rogue, and has been preaching "another gospel," which is no Gospel at all. Religion has perverted the Gospel of the Grace of Christ, and preached a Gospel that is mixing law and grace, teaching people that they are to make monthly payments towards their sin-debt by their behavior, when the truth is JESUS HAS PAID THE SIN DEBT.

You see, by definition, an ambassador is not allowed to convey any message he wants when on assignment. An ambassador is entrusted with a very specific message, and he is given autonomy to convey that message as effectively as possible, but only that message. That is contrary to the very essence of what an ambassador is, yet it is what many preachers have done. They've been entrusted by God to be an ambassador of the ministry of reconciliation, yet they've gone rogue and conveyed another message. They have perverted the Gospel of Christ.

The United States for example has multiple ambassadors assigned to specific nations. If President Obama desires to convey a specific message to Iraq for instance, he informs the U.S. ambassador to Iraq of that message, and entrusts him as an ambassador to convey that message and that message only. The ambassador is given freedom to convey the message in a relatable, effective manner, but the message he was entrusted with must stay intact.

If after arriving in Iraq, the ambassador decides to convey a different message than that which President Obama entrusted him with, he is a very poor ambassador, and he will cause mass confusion. This is what has happened in the church through the veering away from the pure Gospel of the Grace of Christ that God has entrusted us with as ambassadors. Now, we find ourselves so confused and unsure of what the original message was. God is doing an amazing work across the earth as we speak revealing false Gospels, and getting the church back to the original message of the Gospel of the Grace of Christ! Praise God!

I want you to think back to when you first realized your debt had been paid in that hypothetical situation with the big screen payment. How did you feel as you learned you were debt free? As you meditate on the reality of being debt free, an emotion begins to flood your heart. It's called peace.

10
PEACE TREATY

I LIKE TO THINK of peace as a feeling of not being indebted anymore. If you notice in Luke 2:14, we see the Angels declare the manner in which God sent Jesus to the earth:

Luke 2:14 - *"Glory to God in the highest, And on earth PEACE, goodwill toward men!"*

God sent Jesus to declare peace to all men not between men, but between God and man. Allow me to paraphrase what I believe God's declaration to be in Luke 2:14: "Peace, you are not indebted to Me. I know you have been living under a legalistic system in which debt consciousness is the platform from where you think and reason. I declare to you I have sent my son Jesus to establish a new and better system; one that does not perpetuate your debt consciousness, but eradicates it. This new and better system will allow you to finally have freedom in your mind.

It is one where you will be able to reason from the reality that you have no debt before me. My son is going to pay the debt of all people, and liberate their minds from debt consciousness. He is going to pay for the whole world to have no sin debt."

God sent Jesus to declare peace to the world, or in other words, the feeling of not being indebted to the world. This is such great news! I know Jesus was so excited to share this amazing message with the world! What is even more exciting is what Jesus said in John chapter 20. Check this out:

> **John 20: 19-21** – *"Then the same day at evening, being the first day of the week, when the doors were shut where the disciples were assembled for fear of the Jews, came Jesus and stood in the midst, and saith unto them, PEACE BE UNTO YOU. And when he had so said, he shewed unto them his hands and his side. Then were the disciples glad, when they saw the Lord. THEN SAID JESUS TO THEM AGAIN, PEACE BE UNTO YOU: AS MY FATHER HAS SENT ME, EVEN SO SEND I YOU."*

How did God send Jesus? Remember Luke 2:14… God sent Jesus to declare peace! He sent Him carrying the message to the world that they are not indebted, that God did not desire for his precious people to live in the bondage of debt- consciousness. He wanted to take sin debt out of the equation so that He could enter into a true, intimate, love relationship with every person. Jesus declares here in John 20, that in the very same way that God sent

Him into the world declaring Peace, He sends us into the world declaring Peace!

You see, we have not been commissioned by Christ to preach a message that leaves people believing they have to pay their own sin-debt! A message that renders them debt-conscious… Christ has commissioned us in the very same way God commissioned Him: to preach the message that Jesus has already fully paid the sin debt, RECEIVE!! Be debt-free! Stop living in debt-consciousness, and apply the blood of Jesus to your life and your conscience, and be delivered! This is the message of which we are ambassadors.

Remember, an ambassador is entrusted with a specific message. When we deviate from this message of declaring peace to the world, we are no longer ambassadors! The Greek word for peace means, "to join as one again!" Somebody say amen! Religion has gone rogue! It has not been preaching what God wants preached, and mass confusion among Christians has resulted. I want to be part of the answer; I do not want to contribute to the confusion. I want to preach what God wants preached, and that is the Gospel of Peace! I am preaching myself happy!

> **Romans 10:15** - *And how shall they preach, except they be sent? As it is written, 'How beautiful are the feet of them that preach the GOSPEL OF PEACE, and bring glad tidings of good things!'*

Imagine Peter and what he must have been thinking in that room with Jesus in John Chapter 20. Peter had just denied Jesus three times. Peter's guilty conscience was surely eating him alive. He was probably strategizing on the things he could do for Jesus to make up for the sin of denying him not once, or twice, but three times. I bet Peter was planning what good he could do to convince Jesus to approve of him again.

Jesus could sense such things, so before He says anything else, before the conversation goes any further, Jesus knew He needed to create the correct atmosphere in that room of no condemnation, and no sin debt. So, He says to all the disciples, "Peace be unto you." What a beautiful thing to say, and incredibly powerful revealing of the Father's heart. Allow me to paraphrase what that verse means to me: "Guys, I know you're all probably thinking you're indebted to me. None of you even really believed I would rise from the dead. Some of you denied me, and you're sinful conscience is trying to put you back in debt to me. Let me correct you now, before we go any further, and soothe your guilty conscience, and remove the burden of sin debt. Peace be unto you... relax... you are not indebted, and you are forgiven. Understood? Okay, now let's talk."

I am writing myself happy again! Praise the mighty name of Jesus!

11
ENDING THE CYCLE OF MONTHLY PAYMENTS

HOW STRANGE WOULD it be if after you were informed that you were debt-free by that phone representative… after you learned that your balance was paid off and you owed nothing… How strange would it be if you continued to call in each month and make payments despite the reality that you were debt-free? Every time you called, the representative would be thinking, "Why is this person still calling in to make payments? Don't they understand that their debt has been paid?"

This is where religion has left so many Christians. Jesus has paid their debt. They owe nothing. They are debt-free. Yet, they believe they must continue to call in to Heaven, and make payments towards their sin balance as if they had one. They are led to believe they must follow religious rules, regulations, and traditions in order to make timely payments.

Let us see in Jesus name how perverted that is. This

system prevents Christians from even understanding why they worship Jesus, or why they are thankful for Him. It creates an atmosphere of going through the motions, Christians doing what they think they're supposed to, with no real understanding of the majesty and wonderfulness of what Jesus has done for them! They subconsciously believe that Jesus' sacrifice must not have been that great and powerful if they must add to it by their performance. This is exactly what the enemy wants. He wants you feeling alienated like Peter must have felt in that room with Jesus, but God wants you to know you are not alienated in His mind, you are reconciled!

Think about it: If God disqualified people from His life because of the wrong they've done, would God have chosen Peter, the very man who had denied Jesus three times just a few months earlier to give the first post-Pentecost sermon in Acts chapter 2, one of the most powerful sermons in history?! NO! God qualified Peter despite his past, and used Peter in a mighty way! Would God have used David, Moses, or Paul? They are all three murderers!

Peter giving that sermon is such a beautiful picture of how God uses ordinary, flawed people who have missed the mark significantly to do extraordinary things! This can be you too if you just allow God to be merciful to you. It can be difficult to receive God's free gift of mercy if the enemy and a sin conscious mind has been beating you up for a long period of time. However, I believe that as Peter learned to allow Jesus to be merciful to him, you can too! God wants to use you to do extraordinary things in the earth just like He did through Peter, David, Moses, and Paul!

You see, Satan knows the truth that in GOD'S MIND you are loved apart from your sin, valued, cherished, and approved. You are a son, an heir, a priest, a king, you have authority in the earth, you are victorious, etc., but if Satan can convince you of a false reality IN YOUR MIND… one in which you are not any of those things BECAUSE OF YOUR WICKED WORKS, that God disapproves of you and has banished you because of the things you've done, Satan can usher you right out of effortless son-ship and abundant life, and into religious slavery. If you continue to agree with the serpent, and judge yourself by your sin, you will begin the never-ending cycle of tirelessly laboring like a slave to enter back into right-standing with God… to prove to yourself and to God that you are worthy of son-ship. In your mind, you're alienated from the life of God, and an enemy of His because of your wicked works. This is a FALSE REALITY.

The only true reality is that which exists in God's mind. The reality in the mind of God is this: you are a son in whom He is well pleased. You are righteous, blameless, and innocent. Just as I love my precious son Harmon apart from what he can do for me, God loves you apart from your performance. You are loved because you are His child, and you have a rightful place in His house! He wants you in his house! His household is incomplete without you there! Now, will you agree with God? Or agree with the serpent?

Adam agreed with the serpent! Following his sin, Adam began to operate from this thought process. It is the one the serpent tempts every man with, including you, and Jesus Christ Himself, which is this: "You are not a son of God. God's declaration that you are his righteous child is not enough. You are not His son until you do some things to prove you are His son." He tempts you to think like this: "I must define myself not by what God says about me, but by what I can do for Him. I constantly assume God's opinion of me must have changed based on the bad that I've done, so let me do some good in my own ability to satisfy my own conscience, and regain right standing with Him. Surely I have lost my good standing with God based on my actions, so now I must perform to become right again."

This is the "mind of Adam," and it alienates you from God IN YOUR MIND. Remember, the reality in GOD'S MIND is that you are NOT ALIENATED, but RECONCILED. It convinces you that you are an enemy of God IN YOUR MIND, NOT GOD'S. In other words, this is how Adam's mind thought after he fell. The serpent approaches us today just as he did Adam with the very same temptation: to define ourselves by what we can do, not by what God says of us. It is a mind that constantly says to you, "I am not, I must do things to become." It is the voice of the serpent.

12
OH YEA?! PROVE IT!

THE SERPENT APPROACHED Jesus Himself with this same temptation: to define Himself not by what God had declared over Him, which is that He was a son and that God was pleased with Him, but to define Himself by what He could do. He tempted Jesus to buy into the lie that He needed to prove His son-ship before God by the things He could do. Check out the temptation in the wilderness with me from Luke chapter 4:

> **Luke 4:1-3 —** *"And Jesus being full of the Holy Ghost returned from Jordan, and was led by the Spirit into the wilderness, Being forty days tempted of the devil. And in those days he did eat nothing: and when they were ended, he afterward hungered. And the devil said unto him, if thou be the Son of God, command this stone that it be made bread."*

Now, this is one of my very favorite passages of scripture. This passage is actually the reason I named my ministry "Innocence Ministries." Before we get into Satan tempting Jesus just as he did Adam, I first want to exalt the name of my mighty savior Jesus, and shine some light on yet another aspect of his majesty and power!

This passage is a fulfillment of Old Testament prophecy. To be noted, is the fact that Jesus actually fulfilled over 400 Old Testament prophecies to the letter: an undeniable testament to his deity! To put that in perspective, consider that the odds of Jesus perfectly fulfilling only eight prophecies is estimated to be one in ten to the seventeenth power: that is one in 100,000,000,000,000,000. He fulfilled over 400.

In Leviticus chapter 16, we can read about the scapegoat. The scapegoat was a blameless, spotless lamb, which the priest would lay his hands on, signifying the transferring of the sin of all the people onto the innocent lamb, and in the same motion signifying the innocence of the lamb being transferred onto all the people. They would do this every year to atone for the sins of the people. This scapegoat would then be led alive out into the wilderness.

> **Leviticus 16:8-10** – *"Then Aaron shall cast lots for the two goats: one lot for the Lord and the other lot for the scapegoat.* **9** *And Aaron shall bring the goat on which the Lord's lot fell, and offer it as a sin offering.* **10** *But the goat on which the lot fell to be the scapegoat shall be presented alive before the Lord, to make atonement*

upon it, and to let it go as the scapegoat into the wilderness."

The scapegoat of the Old Testament was a type and shadow of the real scapegoat that was to come, which is our Lord Jesus Christ. We arrive thousands of years later, and Jesus, the fulfillment of the scapegoat, is led out into the wilderness, just like the scapegoat in Leviticus 16. Except this time, instead of having to do this repeatedly year after year, Jesus was going to take the sin of the world upon him ONCE AND FOR ALL!! Praise the name of Jesus! IT IS FINISHED!

That was a fun Holy Ghost rabbit trail, but back to the business at hand. Satan's first mistake in the wilderness with Jesus was his assumption that because Jesus was in a weakened physical state (as He had not eaten anything for forty days), Jesus was also in a weakened spiritual state. Ha! Wrong you stupid devil. The devil is an idiot. Jesus was surely very frail physically, but He was still a spiritual POWERHOUSE! Praise the mighty name of Jesus!

Satan's temptation in the garden was to tempt Adam to define himself not by what God had already said about him, but by what he could DO. In verse three, we see Satan approach Jesus with this statement, **"IF you be the Son of God, command this stone to be turned to bread."** Satan attacks Jesus's identity as a son, just as he did Adam. Satan is tempting Jesus to define Himself by what He can do, not by what God has already said. Satan's ploy to Jesus is this: "It is not enough that God has already said you are His son, you must do things to prove your son-ship. You must prove your identity by performing a miracle."

However, JESUS KNEW WHO HE WAS. He was firmly rooted in His identity as a son, and would not fall for the same tricks Adam did. Look what God spoke over Jesus just twenty verses earlier in Luke 3:22!

> **Luke 3:22** – *"And the Holy Ghost descended in a bodily shape like a dove upon him, and a voice came from heaven, which said, Thou art my beloved Son; in thee I am well pleased."*

God had JUST PUBICLY DECLARED the son-ship of Jesus, and that HE WAS WELL PLEASED WITH JESUS! Yet still, the devil comes and tempts Jesus to forget what God had just said, and define Himself not by what God spoke over Him, but by the miracles he could do. This is the serpent tempting Jesus to think like Adam. He is tempting a son to think like a slave.

He may be attacking you with this same temptation right now. Let's use the authority we have in the name of Jesus, and together let's command the enemy to leave right now:

> **"Devil, you have no right to attack my mind. I am a son of the most high God in whom He is well pleased all the time, no matter what. I reject your lies. I will not think like a slave. I am a beloved son/daughter. I know who I am. I do not need to do anything to prove it either. Thank you Jesus!"**

James 4:7 – *"Therefore submit to God. Resist the devil and HE WILL FLEE from you."*

Luke 10:19 – *"Behold, I give unto you power to tread on serpents and scorpions, and over all the power of the enemy: and nothing shall by any means hurt you."*

13
YOU HAVE BEEN PREAPPROVED

NOW, YOU MUST see, that Jesus was yet to minister a single day when God spoke those words over Him, that He was WELL PLEASED with Jesus, for all to hear! Jesus was yet to do anything for God! Yet, God declares how pleased He is with Him before He does anything. Don't you see?! God does not need you to do anything for Him, or minister a single day for Him to declare publicly that HE IS PLEASED WITH YOU!

God's main concern is not what you can do for Him; it is TO KNOW YOU, and for you to know how pleased He already is with you! Remember the definition of Agape that we covered earlier. Part of the definition was, "To be well pleased with." God is well pleased with you before you ever do anything for Him, for His love has nothing to do with your performance. Jesus' understanding of this, that He was a son already, that God was pleased with Him already, before He ever did anything for God, was actually what fueled His ministry! It is not the other way around. We do not minister to earn son-ship... we minister because we know we are already sons, and we are secure in that, and we want to invite others into this beautiful family reality that exists already between God and us.

The more you meditate on how pleased He is with you without you doing anything for Him, the more you'll want to do for Him. That's how the love of God works. Knowing God loves you produces good works; good works don't produce the knowledge of God's love... huge difference!

If you've given into the serpent's temptation of trying to get you to do something to become what you already are, and therefore have begun to think like Adam, legalistic Christianity can be very enticing to you. It will provide you with a tangible set of rules to follow, or tasks you can perform, to begin defining your worthiness and regaining son-ship by what you can do. Legalism steps in to provide for the mind of Adam. We think, *"Yes, I can follow that list of things, and it'll be great, because I'll have a way to measure my holiness and worthiness to be considered a son before God." "I am a son because I never miss a tithe. I am a son because I've volunteered in the choir twice a week for 30 years. I am a son because I wear an earpiece and work security on Sundays."*

That is spiritual quicksand. It is exactly what the serpent desires for you. We incorrectly see ourselves as, "I am not, I must do things to become," so naturally, when a preacher gives us a list of things we can do, we jump all over it so we can begin doing things to become, when the whole time we ALREADY ARE!!! Just like Adam, we have already been made complete! Let us not fall into the same deception he did, and buy into the serpent's lie that we are not, we must become! It will kill us just like it killed Adam! Believing this lie will change our actions. It will cause us to climb on the religious hamster wheel, and enter into the cycle of trying to earn things from God that He has already declared are free.

We have been given, and are designed to think from the "mind of Christ," which is a mind that constantly says to us, *"I am because God says I am. I am his child not because of what I can do, but because God says I am, end of story, I have life and peace."* Legalism frustrates the mind of Christ. If you are thinking like a Son as you're designed to, you will no longer entertain a legalistic slave mindset. You will set foot in a legalistic atmosphere and immediately want to get out. Realizing you are a beloved son or daughter of God, in whom He is always well pleased, will totally change your life. This revelation has the power to resurrect you, whereas thinking like Adam will kill you.

> **1 Cor 2:16 –** *"For who has known the mind of the Lord, that he may instruct him? BUT WE HAVE THE MIND OF CHRIST."*

Adam tragically began to believe that because of what he'd done, God's feelings towards him had changed, so he went and hid. All manner of incorrect thoughts began attacking him. He believed a lie he formed in his own guilty conscience that God was angry or disappointed with him based on his poor performance, then this belief led to the action of covering himself with a prickly, uncomfortable fig leaf and hiding from God.

Religion and legalism causes us to cover up with fig leaves just as Adam did. We try and cover up the imperfections we see in ourselves based on which rules we've failed to adhere to. We get to church and act like everything's perfect. We run into a fellow church member at Starbuck's and pretend we're doing great, and we're on fire for God, when we're actually exhausted, and our flame is burning low. The superficiality that results from legalism will absolutely wear you out. You're not designed to pretend all the time. You're not designed to hide behind a fig leaf all day. You are designed to simply "be." You are designed in God's image to have peace, and to enjoy life. That is the mind of Christ; the mind that says, *"I have no reason to cover up with a fig leaf. I am because God says I am. He approves of me already! I am complete and lacking nothing!"*

14
STEPPING OUT FROM BEHIND THE FIG LEAF

THE RELIGIOUS, FIG leaf-Christian life is not what God has planned for you... it is not the abundant life Jesus wants for you. In case you didn't know, everyone can see your fig leaves: we can see you hiding and hurting behind them. It is okay, I have been there.

Grace is amazing because it reveals the needlessness of the exhausting fig leaves of superficial Christianity. Grace heals you from the wounds that superficial Christianity has left behind, and empowers you to just "be." Grace creates the atmosphere of safety you need to step out from behind the fig leaf. Grace equips you to live in peace, freedom, and son-ship as Adam did before he fell. These wounds become part of your testimony of deliverance from religion, rather than what defines and limits you.

I want to show you how God feels about the fig leaf existence in which so many of His precious children are living. He does not approve! He wants his kids to live in the reality of what Jesus has provided: freedom and effortless son-ship! Let's read this passage together in Matthew, where Jesus curses the fig tree:

> **Matt. 21:17-20** – *"And He left them, and went out of the city into Bethany; and He lodged there. Now in the morning as He returned into the city, He was hungry {an hungered}. And when He saw a fig tree in the way, He came to it, and found nothing thereon, but leaves only, and said unto it, "Let no fruit grow on thee henceforward forever." And presently the fig tree withered away. And when the disciples saw it, they marveled, saying, "How soon is the fig tree withered away!"*

Now there is some powerful symbolism going on here that I want you to see. First of all, Jesus was hungry. He needed sustenance. Jesus spots a fig tree in his way and enthusiastically approaches it expecting to be nourished, only to discover there to be no fruit upon it. There was only the appearance of fruit from afar.

The fig tree represents the lifeless, legalistic, religious church that is mixing law with Grace. It represents the church that teaches believers to think like Adam. The church that is so prevalent today, which is mixing the lethal cocktail of the tree of life (Jesus), with the tree of the knowledge of good and evil (legalism). It represents the powerless legalistic system of religion, which mass-produces Christians who have no victory. Christians who like Adam, feel condemned, ashamed, and unworthy, and are covering up with fig leaves. Christians who have no understanding that they are already sons and daughters of God, unconditionally loved and approved!

Now, from a distance, this "fig tree" appears tasty and promising. Just as Jesus spotted the fig tree from afar, and thought He'd found a way to satisfy his hunger, people look at the church from the outside and say, "I'm hungry for God, I need sustenance, let me go to this church and I shall be fed." Upon closer examination however, you realize that there is nothing there to feed you. There is only disappointment and frustration. There are only bitter, prickly leaves there. You realize religion is breeding people that think like Adam… that they're never worthy, and they must constantly earn, earn, earn, and perform, perform, perform, to convince God of their worthiness for son-ship.

When Jesus curses the fig tree, He is cursing this legalistic system I'm describing. He is cursing the church that exalts rules, regulations, and traditions above leading people into an intimate relationship with God. He is cursing the system that teaches you must add to Jesus's sacrifice by your performance. He is cursing the system that teaches the mind of Adam that you are not what God says you are, that you are not as you ought to be, and you must do things to become what you ought to be. He is displaying His utter disapproval of it.

This system hurts God's children. This system causes God's children to live a quality of life far below what He desires for them. This system yields superficiality, and exhausts God's children. This system leads to a wrong perception of the heart of God! As a loving father, this makes him angry! God passionately loves His children, and does not enjoy seeing them live without peace and victory!

Jesus discovering that the fig tree had no nourishment is a picture of us discovering that religion has no nourishment. Religion cannot feed you; it will only deplete you. Religion is not the bread of life, and religion is not the manna from heaven that nourishes God's people. On the contrary, Jesus is the bread of life, and Jesus is the manna from heaven that nourishes God's people! Just like the manna in the Old Testament, there is plenty of Jesus to feed everyone! Religion and Jesus are not synonyms; they are antonyms. They are opposites! One depletes, and the other nourishes. One kills, and the other gives life!

Jesus cursing the fig tree is also a picture of how with one touch from Jesus, that religious, legalistic way of thinking that has provided no nourishment for you for all these years is cursed! When your mind gets a touch from Jesus and begins to understand the Grace of God, and the finished work of Jesus on the Cross, your legalistic thought processes begin to wither away and die just like the fig tree! The thought process that has been yielding death in your life begins to get uprooted by the truth of God's Grace and removed for good! Glory to God!

This touch from Jesus, this revelation of Grace, is so powerful that just as the disciples did, you will marvel at how quickly the fig tree in your mind will wither away! Your spirit will resonate as the truth invades your heart and mind. Excitement for God will return! You will feel nourished again. The power of God will destroy the incorrect thoughts religion has taught you, and replace them with correct thoughts of love, approval, peace, and freedom! Praise His name!

The bible is full of passages like this displaying that God's true heart is one of Love and Grace, not law and condemnation… but we have always read these passages through the lens of the mind of Adam, thinking "God is disappointed and angry with us," instead of through the lens of the ministry of Jesus and the mind of Christ, which displays that "God is not angry with us, He's not out to get us, we are his children, and He has good news for us!"

15
CONQUERING THE GOLIATH OF PERFORMANCE MINDEDNESS

LET'S CHECK OUT the story of David and Goliath for more illustration of how powerful a revelation of Grace is in destroying incorrect thought patterns. Here are ten verses from 1 Sam. 17 out of the Message bible to review before getting into the good news:

> **1 Sam. 17: 40-51** – *"Then David took his shepherd's staff, selected five smooth stones from the brook, and put them in the pocket of his shepherd's pack, and with his sling in his hand approached Goliath. As the Philistine paced back and forth, his shield bearer in front of him, he noticed David. He took one look down on him and sneered—a mere youngster, apple-cheeked*

and peach-fuzzed. The Philistine ridiculed David. "Am I a dog that you come after me with a stick?" And he cursed him by his gods. "Come on," said the Philistine. "I'll make roadkill of you for the buzzards. I'll turn you into a tasty morsel for the field mice." David answered, "You come at me with sword and spear and battle-ax. I come at you in the name of God-of-the-Angel-Armies, the God of Israel's troops, whom you curse and mock. This very day God is handing you over to me. I'm about to kill you, cut off your head, and serve up your body and the bodies of your Philistine buddies to the crows and coyotes. The whole earth will know that there's an extraordinary God in Israel. And everyone gathered here will learn that God doesn't save by means of sword or spear. The battle belongs to God—he's handing you to us on a platter!" That roused the Philistine, and he started toward David. David took off from the front line, running toward the Philistine. David reached into his pocket for a stone, slung it, and hit the Philistine hard in the forehead, embedding the stone deeply. The Philistine crashed, facedown in the dirt. That's how David beat the Philistine— with a sling and a stone. He hit him and killed him. No sword for David! Then David ran up to the Philistine and stood over him, pulled the giant's sword from its sheath, and finished the job by cutting off his head. When the Philistines saw that their great champion was dead, they scattered, running for their lives. The men of Israel and Judah were up on their feet, shouting!"

Notice that David picks up five stones from the brook. The number five represents Grace in the bible. David didn't pick up five stones because he thought he might miss with the first four. David picking up five stones is God giving us a picture of His Grace. It is a picture of the ability of God's Grace to empower us unto victory against what in the natural world, is a seemingly insurmountable foe. When we are armed with a revelation of Grace as David was, we have unshakable boldness and victory as he did!

Sometimes in the natural world we encounter "Goliath" situations and circumstances… ones that if we view them with only natural eyes, we can be stricken with fear just as Saul and Saul's army were… but God's grace is more than sufficient to bring victory over any Goliath the enemy tries to put in our way! It just took one little teenage, pretty boy, red-head armed with the weapon of God's grace to lead an army stricken with fear against a seemingly undefeatable foe. God is revealing pictures of the immeasurable power of His grace even way back in this time of David.

Armed with the five stones of Grace, David is emboldened to run directly and fearlessly towards his enemy, not to cower away riddled with fear. Grace will cause you to go forward through your Goliath situation with boldness. David shoots and strikes a direct hit in the forehead of Goliath with the very first shot. The shot has such accuracy and velocity that it embeds in Goliath's forehead and levels him instantly! This is a picture of how one

Grace-thought, embedded in your mind, has the power to topple the goliath of legalistic thinking.

I can boldly testify in my own life that this is true! I remember getting a hold of **John 1:17**, which says, *"the law came by Moses, but Grace and Truth came by Jesus Christ,"* and thinking on that one verse for a month at least. My wrong views of God, and myself, began to whither away just from the Grace and Truth contained in that one thought! The verse embedded itself in my forehead… in the forefront of my mind. I began to see that truth is attached to Grace, not law! Truth comes through understanding Grace, not understanding legalism! Law brings fear, Grace chases fear out and births supernatural boldness like David displayed. The Goliath of my legalistic thinking was being leveled! I began to have joy, and smile when I thought about God, instead of getting burdened every time I thought about God.

After Goliath was leveled by the Grace stone, David climbed on top of him and decapitated Goliath with his own sword, symbolizing the end result of a revelation of Grace: the legalistic mind being completely removed! Grace will decapitate the mind of obligation, unworthiness, guilt, shame, and condemnation, and will regenerate a mind full of freedom, love, acceptance, peace, and Grace. Glory to God!

After the Philistines saw their Giant lying lifeless and decapitated on the battlefield, they all fled running for their lives. This is a picture of how legalistic thinking is the "giant" that the enemy and his minions need to intimidate you. When these powers of darkness see that a revelation of Grace has decapitated the Goliath of your legalistic mind, they realize they have no power to rule over you… no way to keep you intimidated… they see their Goliath lying lifeless on the battlefield of your mind. They see that you are now armed with a mighty revelation of Grace, and they can never stand against you again!

Just as the Philistines saw they could not stand against David as he was armed with Grace, and they ran for their lives, the powers of the enemy to bring shame, condemnation, and guilt know they can no longer stand against you when you understand God's Grace, and they flee for their lives!

Finally, we must take note that David picked up five Grace stones from the brook, but only needed one. That means he had four leftover in his satchel. The supply of God's Grace will always be greater than your need. This is why the Bible says there is an "abundance of Grace." It's why the bible says, "where sin abounds, Grace does much more abound!" The supply of God's Grace for you ALWAYS far exceeds your need! There is always Grace leftover. You cannot exhaust His continual supply of Grace! You will always have stones left in your satchel! Glory to God!

Glory and honor to the mighty name of Jesus! I am writing myself happy. I am so thankful for Jesus and the life-changing power of His Amazing Grace!

16
THOUGHT LEASHES

I BELIEVE GOD REFERRED to David as, "a man after His own heart" because David understood God's Grace before his time. David never claimed to be perfect, but knew he could run to God for mercy when he had made a mistake, and this pleased God.

Now, in the New Testament, Paul received a revelation of Grace directly from Jesus, and He was gifted with an ability to teach and relate this revelation to us. Check out how Paul articulates the different things that will manifest in our lives based on how we are thinking and believing. Paul explains what manifests when we are thinking with the legalistic fig tree mindset, aka the "mind of Adam," and when we're thinking with the Grace, or tree of life mindset, aka the "mind of Christ:"

> **Romans 8:6** – *"For to be carnally minded is death; but to be spiritually minded is life and peace."*

Read that verse carefully… this is very radical. Notice, Paul does not say, "to be carnally acting is death, and to be spiritually acting is life and peace." Why not? You may be thinking, *"I thought I needed to act spiritual, and act holy, and that's how I stay good with God. My whole Christian walk is about me focusing on behaving like a good Christian should."*

Don't misunderstand me, acting holy and spiritually is certainly good; but not as a means to earn God's love and approval. If you see your behavior as a means to earn from God, you will never have peace. You will never get off the religious hamster wheel. You will never be thankful. You will live in a place of perpetual frustration and negative self-opinion. Your conscience will never stop telling you, "The job is not done. You have more work to do." You will always think God is extending and retracting his love yo-yo from you based on your performance. You will be reaching for fig leaves all the time to cover yourself up. This is the bondage so many Christians live in.

The truth is, acting holy is an effortless FRUIT of BELIEVING CORRECTLY. It is not an effort to enter into God's love; it is a fruit of knowing you are already loved. It is not a means to earn holy status; it is the fruit of knowing you've already been freely given holy status.

Paul understood what you and I are discussing: that an action simply reveals the belief that led to the action. The belief is the root, and the action is the fruit. So, we now see the importance of hearing correct teaching, because correct teaching will lead to correct believing, which will lead to life and peace! This is God's will! He takes no pleasure in you having no peace. It breaks His heart as a loving Father.

This is why Paul said to be carnally MINDED is death, not carnally acting. Paul is dealing with the root. Ask yourself, if you want to remove a weed in your yard, do you merely cut the weed above the surface of the ground? No, you must go beneath the surface of the ground and dig up the root to ensure it is being permanently removed.

Paul is stating that when we incorrectly believe we must earn God's love and approval through our behavior, and maintain it through our behavior, we are living in CARNAL MINDEDNESS. When we are sin conscious, always being mindful of how we've come up short, rather than allowing the blood of Jesus to wash our conscience in innocence, we are living in CARNAL MINDEDNESS. We are thinking with the mind of Adam instead of the mind of Christ. We are believing INCORRECTLY, and all manner of death, depression, anxiety, unrest, exhaustion, bitterness, confusion, shame, etc. will manifest in our lives!

But, when we are spiritually minded, when we think from the mind of Christ... in other words, when we believe correctly that Jesus was enough, that we no longer need to be sin conscious (constantly mindful of what we've done wrong, or how we've come up short), but righteousness conscious (mindful that we are forever right with God through Jesus' work on the Cross), that our behavior is not our savior, but Jesus is our savior, that God's love for us is unconditional and not based on how holy we can act or how well we can perform for him, that sonship is our reality, we are BELIEVING CORRECTLY! Life, peace, joy, and contentment will begin to manifest in our lives!

> **Hebrews 10:2** - *For then would they not have ceased to be offered? (continual sin sacrifices as they were performed in the Old Testament) because that the worshippers once purged should have had NO MORE CONSCIOUSNESS OF SINS.*

> **Romans 5:17** - *For if by the one man's offense death reigned through the one, much more those who receive abundance (remember the 4 stones david had leftover) of grace and of the GIFT OF RIGHTEOUSNESS (it's a GIFT, not something to be earned!) will reign in life through the One, Jesus Christ.*

17

LEGALISM: THE SILENT ASSASSIN

THE CHURCH AS a whole is far too focused on correcting behavior. Focusing on correcting behavior is like trying to remove a weed by only cutting it above the surface of the ground. The church needs to focus on correcting beliefs, for that is what will correct behavior; that is the root. This is what will lead to life and peace dominating the lives of believers.

We need leaders who believe correctly, so that they can teach their congregations to believe correctly. We need leaders leading people into their own relationship with God, not a relationship that goes through the middleman of the pastor. Subsequently, the proper behavior will follow when these proper beliefs are taught, and take root in people.

So, the question now becomes what belief teaches us to behave like representatives of Heaven should behave? What belief is the key to bringing forth the fruit of living clean and holy like we never could using our own fleshly willpower to act holy under legalism and religion? GRACE GRACE GRACE!!!

Now, I know what you might be thinking: *"I've always been taught that Grace is a license to sin. I probably should stay away from that."* Fair enough… but realize, that is the same objection Paul encountered when he unashamedly preached the true Gospel of Grace. The position that Grace is a license to sin, which is born from ignorance, causes many pastors to stay away from pure New Covenant Grace teaching, and continue to preach a mixture of grace and legalism. They mix the old and new covenants in an attempt to "keep their congregations in check, " not realizing they're actually conjuring up a lethal cocktail of Grace and Law, strengthening sin in people's lives, and preventing people from experiencing victory.

Let's go ahead and deal with this age-old objection, and settle it in our hearts once and for all that PURE Grace is the only avenue for true victory for the believer, not a license to stay in sin. Legalism is what causes people to say bound in sin, not Grace. Look what Paul says about the lethal powers of legalism in 2 Cor. 3:5-6:

> **2 Cor 3:5-6** – *"Not that we are sufficient of ourselves to think of anything as being from ourselves, but our sufficiency is from God, who also made us sufficient as ministers of the new covenant, not of the letter but of the Spirit;[a] for the letter (legalism) KILLS , but the Spirit (Jesus, Grace) gives life."*

Legalism kills. Grace plus law is a toxic mixture that kills people, and prevents believers from experiencing victory, further life and peace, and a vibrant personal relationship with Jesus. Picture that you have 100 oz. of liquid. Ninety nine oz. of this liquid is harmless, life-giving water (Grace), and 1 oz. is deadly poison (law).

Even though this cocktail is 99% life giving, the reality is it still has the power to prevent further life. The truth is that even though the poison only comprises 1 % of the cocktail, this poison unto death is still present! As long as the life giving water remains mixed with this poison unto death, it's still a deadly mixture. Despite the 99 oz. of life giving water, the lingering presence of the 1 oz. of deadly poison mixes a deadly cocktail. However, if we can extract the 1 oz. of poison unto death, now we are left with 100% pure, life-giving water. Jesus is the pure life giving water. He is the "still water" David references in Psalm 23.

> **Psalm 23:1-2** - *The Lord is my shepherd; I shall not want. He makes me to lie down in green pastures: he leads me beside the still waters.*

God is shepherding the flock of his children towards the life giving, still water of Jesus Christ. God will not shepherd his flock of precious children towards poisonous waters. This is why churches that teach a mixture of law and Grace are dying. It is because God is a good shepherd, and He loves his sheep... He will not lead them to drink of poisonous waters.

18
THE PATRIOT MISSILE OF GOD'S LOVE

GOD IS IN the business of removing "that which kills." He is not a perverse God, who gets a kick out of watching his children ingest "that which kills," even if they're only ingesting tiny amounts. "That which kills," is the deadly cocktail of Law and Grace.

My son Harmon is 18 months old now, and right after he began walking, he discovered how to get into our kitchen cabinets. He was, and still is one lightning fast, active little guy! However, before Harmon was ever able to even walk, Michelle and I foresaw a need to remove "that which kills" from all those floor level cabinets. We could foresee that soon he would be tall enough, strong enough, and mobile enough to get into those cabinets.

Just as God loves us, and takes extreme effort to protect us from "that which kills," which is the mixture of law and grace, Michelle and I took extreme effort to remove anything that could hurt Harmon from those kitchen cabinets. We made provision for his safety and freedom by removing that which kills. We made absolutely sure there were no harmful or deadly chemicals, knives, forks, extremely heavy items, or anything at all inside the cabinets that could ever hurt him. We removed "that which kills."

Now, we did this because we wanted him to be able to enjoy an atmosphere of freedom… one where he was free to open the cabinets as he pleased, but have no chance of hurting himself. My precious little man loved this atmosphere of freedom! It was such a joy to watch him.

You see, as human beings, we are made in the image of God, and are designed to be free as God is. We enjoy life most in freedom. The Christian life is not exempt from this aspect of our design. Our Christian walk is supposed to be enjoyed in freedom too!

Harmon absolutely loves opening and closing those cabinets; he has a blast! As his father who loves him, I thoroughly enjoy watching him have so much fun, and operate in such freedom. I do not have to chase him around yelling "no!" every time he goes to open a cabinet, for that which kills has been completely removed.

The bible teaches that the law is the strength of sin (1 Cor 15:56), so every time I would say no to him, it would revive the law that says he is not allowed to open the cabinets, which would only feed and strengthen his desire to open them! I would be creating a never-ending cycle where his desire to "sin" by opening the cabinet would never die! This is a picture of a Christian trying to overcome sin by following rules. It is an approach that is bound to fail.

Now, because there is no law present for Harmon that says, "thou shalt not open the cabinets," opening them is not even especially attractive to him anymore. To him, there is no forbidden aspect to opening the cabinets. So, after he spent a few weeks being obsessed with opening them, now he occasionally remembers that he enjoys it, but for the most part leaves them alone entirely. He is free from that particular "sin," and not because he's learned to follow a law by his own willpower, but through the complete removal of that law, and the introduction of freedom in a safe atmosphere.

However, if that law were present saying He could not open them, the attraction to open them would never wane. It would awaken in him the desire to open the cabinets each time he remembered he was not supposed to. The law is the strength of sin.

1 Cor 15:56 – *"The sting of death is sin; and the strength of sin is the law."*

19
PICKET FENCES

NOT LONG AGO, I was in a local Pastor's meeting. I have been attending them in an attempt to bring unity among pastors and believers in my community. My community has 98 churches, and less than 6,000 people that go to church. It is very divided. Different churches refuse to minister together because they are under the deception that if you don't agree completely with someone, you cannot love them, get along with them, or minister alongside them. This is a deception of the enemy.

100% agreement is not prerequisite to loving someone. We all love people in our own families and circles of friends whom we don't agree with on everything! Nevertheless, doctrinally, most churches believe we must agree on every single thing before we can minister together. Rubbish! Here's how the conversation should go: "Do we agree that Jesus is the Son of God, the spotless lamb who died for the sins of all people, and that God raised Him from the dead? Yes? Okay, well let's go love on some people together!"

Do you know that even if you speak in tongues, and your Baptist brother down the street thinks tongues are not for today, you guys can still minister together? Do you agree that Jesus is the Son of God, and God raised Him from the dead? Do you agree that people need Jesus? Okay, then you can minister together.

Do you know that even if you don't think God heals anymore, and Pentecostal Pattie down the street prays for people to be healed every week, that you two can still minister together? You see, you and Pentecostal Pattie agree that Jesus is the Son of God, and God raised Him from the dead, and that people need Jesus, so put aside such a nonessential difference in opinion and go minister together! How long are we going to stay hung up on nonessential differences?

I like to call these differences "picket fence doctrines." Picture you are a tongue-talking, healing believing Pentecostal, and you have a back yard with a waste high, picket fence at your house. Now, on a Saturday afternoon you are outside in the back yard tilling the ground for your spring garden. As you're working, your non-tongue talking, non-healing believing next-door neighbor Presbyterian Pam also comes outside to work in their yard. She is just on the other side of the fence from you, literally and doctrinally.

Now, ask yourself, can you two still converse in the presence of the picket fence separating you? Does this picket fence totally prevent you two from communicating and having a great conversation? Does this fence prevent you from helping each other? Could you not easily climb over the picket fence, overcoming all that separates you, and give Presbyterian Pam a hug? Could you not climb over that little fence and pray for her to be comforted as she lost a loved one recently? Can you not find any common ground despite the presence of the picket fence?

Absolutely you can! See, Christians are believing a lie. This lie says that these picket fence doctrinal differences are actually 10-foot thick, concrete wall doctrines that we cannot communicate through. Stupidity! This is just what the devil wants. He wants us to exist in loveless, powerless division in the church. Let us realize we can absolutely find common ground, encourage each other, and minister TOGETHER, IN UNITY, despite the picket fences that separate our doctrinal views.

20
THE UNITY ANOINTING AND CONFIDENCE IN THE TRUTH

YOU SEE, THE Bible is profoundly clear on the power of unity, and the powerlessness of division. Look what David declares in Psalm 133, and let's learn about how powerful unity is in the body of Christ:

Psalm 133: - *"Behold, how good and how pleasant it is for brethren to dwell together in unity! It is like the precious ointment (anointing oil) upon the head, that ran down upon the beard, even Aaron's beard: that went down to the skirts of his garments; As the dew of Hermon, and as the dew that descended upon the mountains of Zion: for there (Zion) the Lord commanded the blessing, even life for evermore."*

Psalm 133 teaches that it is beautiful for brethren to dwell together in UNITY, and that the anointing flows through UNITY. Conversely, this means that it's not beautiful for brethren to dwell in division, and that there is no anointing when division is prevalent.

The next aspect of this passage is incredibly powerful. Psalm 133 also teaches that God commands His blessing on Mt. Zion, not Mt. Sinai. Mt. Zion is representative of God's Grace, and Mt. Sinai is representative of Old Testament law. Remember, the law was given on Mt. Sinai. According to scripture, there is no blessing commanded by God upon the teaching of law. The blessing of God is commanded on the teaching of Grace. So, if you are teaching law, there is no anointing, and there is no blessing from God.

This is very near to God's heart. The enemy has brought division through denominations because he is aware of the power of unity. Satan was listening when Jesus said in Mark chapter 3: "a kingdom divided against itself cannot stand." I believe when he heard Jesus say that, he set out to divide Christians worldwide and he has mostly succeeded. Division causes a cracked, wobbly kingdom foundation.

Think about Paul's New Testament letters. Have you ever noticed that Paul's letters are not addressed to denominations? The letters are simply addressed to, "The Church at Philippi, or The Church at Corinth." Paul does not write letters addressed to, "The Methodist church at Philippi, or the Baptist church at Corinth." His letters are addressed to ONE CHURCH. Unified.

Denominational division came through Satan taking

the opportunity to manipulate through man's need to control people, and man's need to be right. It did not come from God. This desire to control people and to be right is not a Godly desire. God already knows He's right, and is not so insecure that He needs everyone to agree with Him for Him to settle it in His heart that He's right. He is also secure enough that He desires freedom for His kids. He does not want to be a nagging micromanager.

Ask yourself; do you need people to agree with you for you to believe you're right? Are you always trying to control people? Do you find that you avoid people that you're aware don't agree with you on everything? I'm not talking about your closest friends; they most likely are like-minded, and that is great. I'm referring to people in general, people outside your inner circle; do you avoid those who disagree with you? If so, you may not have settled it in your own heart that what you believe is truth. Confidence that what you believe is the truth reduces the fear of being disagreed with, for you know you are unshakably rooted in the truth. This is why Peter said in **1 Peter 3:15**, *"But in your hearts revere Christ as Lord. Always be prepared to give an answer to everyone who asks you to give the reason for the hope that you have. But do this with gentleness and respect."*

Peter even mentioning this shows that as believers, we are called to spend time around people who might ask us to give reason why we believe that Christ is the truth. Now, don't misunderstand me… there is immense value in having fellowship with like-minded believers and being part of a local church; I am not diminishing that. It is SO IMPORTANT to have community with like-minded believers. But, I am saying that we are not called to be separatists, and ONLY spend time around people who think exactly like we do. We are not called to be sequestered like the jurors at the O.J. trial.

In reality, the more you settle it in your heart that Christ is in fact the way and the truth, the more ready and willing you'll be to share your personal story of what Christ has done for you, and why you believe He is the Truth, even to a skeptical unbeliever who you know doesn't agree!

If you already know God unconditionally accepts you, you no longer have any fear of rejection from others! You can just be the authentic you without any fear of disagreement or rejection! My good friend Pastor Jeremiah Johnson from Grace Point Church in Georgetown, KY says it like this; "You don't have to be fake when you're not afraid of being rejected."

Let me comfort you, Jesus and His Grace IS THE TRUTH! Jesus came full of Grace and Truth! Grace and Truth came by Jesus Christ! (Jn 1:14-18, 29) Searching for truth and searching for Jesus are the same thing. If we only spend time with people who are exactly like-minded, we will shine our lights only on each other and blind ourselves! Our lights are meant to shine outside the church, and in the darkness as well!

Agreement from others should not be a prerequisite for you to be confident in what you believe. Truth will be engrafted into your belief system whenever you agree with God. The Holy Spirit will resonate within you when you hear the glorious truth of what God says about you, and this resonance will lead you to agree with the truth you're hearing. Jesus said in John 16:13, *"However, when he, the Spirit of truth, is come, he will guide you into all truth."*

He will settle it within you supernaturally. This happens when the Holy Spirit hears Jesus, not man, being exalted, when Grace is being preached. When that happens, you no longer have an insecure need for others to always agree with you in order for you to have confidence that the message of Grace is the Truth. When you've tasted the freedom of knowing the truth, which comes only by being fed the nourishing manna of Jesus Christ, you will not accept anything less from that point forward!

21
CARBS ARE GREAT WHEN THEY COME FROM THE BREAD OF LIFE!

SO, BACK TO the meeting... about an hour and a half into this meeting, these area pastors began to discuss why so many churches in the area are dying. I had not yet spoken in the meeting, as my goal is to integrate, and unify with these area pastors as seamlessly as possible. I am trying to learn from, and earn the respect of these much older men, so I did not want to come into my first meeting and talk too much! I had decided I was really there to just listen.

As they began to discuss why churches are dying, I felt the Holy Spirit beginning to do backflips on the inside of me. God was giving me something to say, and as the Holy Spirit unpacked it for me, I began to realize how very radical sounding it would be to these gentlemen. I selfishly hoped they would not ask me to chime in. But sure enough, they eventually turned to me and asked, "Jake, since you're a newcomer with a little more of an outside perspective, we're interested to hear your take on this."

I started to answer, and at first I attempted to dance around what God had given me to say, but I knew He wanted me to share it, and I couldn't avoid it forever. Eventually, I relented and submitted to the Holy Spirit. I presented to the other pastors the question God had presented to me.

I said, "Gentlemen, how long would it take the people of Ashland (KY, where I live) to stop going out to eat, if at every single restaurant they got food poisoning?" A confused look came across all their faces. They asked me to say it again, and I did, and then they asked me what I meant.

I said, "Guys, God loves his children with a passionate love, and as a good father, he will not lead his children to eat from a poisonous tree, or to drink from poisonous waters. The churches here have been preaching a lethal mixture of law and grace for so many decades, that they are all dying. A little bit of poison ingested regularly will kill you slowly over time. God will simply not lead his children towards poison, towards a lethal cocktail of law and grace. We need to start preaching 100% Grace, 100% Jesus again, and the churches will come back to life, because God can lead his children there again with confidence."

As I was releasing this Word, you could feel the presence of God fill the room… man it was so thick and powerful. I started to boldly declare, "We must exalt the mighty name of Jesus! We must stop exalting man! We must lead people not to a man, a pastor, but to Jesus! We must feed people the manna from Heaven who is Jesus Christ, not the lethal mixture of the tree of life and the tree of the knowledge of good and evil!" As I was finishing up, this elderly pastor started to prophecy out of nowhere! He had not said a single word the entire meeting!

As soon as we started saying and exalting the name of Jesus, the Holy Spirit had something to work within that meeting! Remember, Jesus said, "the Holy Spirit shall testify of ME." If we're not preaching Jesus, or exalting Jesus, the Holy Spirit has no one of whom He can testify! It was so powerful in there!

Remember, Jesus said, "When I am lifted up, I will draw all men to myself." We must stop lifting man up, and trying to draw people to worship the "man of God." We must begin lifting Jesus up, and He will draw men to Himself as He said He would! A real man of God does not lead people to himself; a true man of God leads people to Jesus.

This old gentleman laid hands on me not knowing me at all, and began to prophecy! He read my mail exactly, everything he said resonated with my spirit and was encouraging! It was so powerful! I was crying, and the other pastors were shouting with joy as the Holy Spirit reminded them of the mighty power in the name of Jesus!! Glory to God!! I thanked that old guy from the bottom of my heart, and weeks later He invited me to preach in His church! Only God can do things like that...

The Gospel of Grace always exalts Jesus, and therefore creates an atmosphere for the Holy Spirit to move and touch people's hearts and feed them what they need to be nourished. His very design is to testify of Jesus. The more legalism and man worship there is in the church, and the more people's behavior is the focus, the less Jesus is exalted. The power of God will flow in a church to the degree that the name of Jesus is being exalted. This is why Grace is so amazing… it ALWAYS exalts JESUS!

There will always be power present to heal, deliver, and liberate when Grace is being preached because it will always exalt the King of Kings, the name above all names, the mighty name of Jesus! The preaching of Grace is all about the work of Jesus Christ, not the work of man. Law preaching focuses on what man can do in his own ability, instead of focusing on the work Christ has already done on behalf of man. Focusing on man is not the Gospel. It does not create an atmosphere for the power of God to flow freely.

22
DISTILLING THE 200 PROOF GOSPEL

WE MUST SETTLE it in our hearts that Grace is the only true Gospel. We must gain knowledge that this Gospel of the Grace of Christ is the power of God to save the world.

> **Romans: 1:16** – *"For I am not ashamed of the Gospel of Christ, for it (this Gospel of Grace) is the POWER (dunamis- miracle working power) of God unto Salvation (soteria – complete wholeness and deliverance in every area)!"*

In fact, according to the scripture, any other Gospel is inherently accursed. Look at the radical statement Paul makes here in Galations 1:6-9:

> **Galatians 1:6-9**: *I marvel that ye are so soon removed from him that called you into the*

grace of Christ unto another gospel: Which is not another; but there be some that trouble you, and would pervert the gospel of Christ. But though we, or an angel from heaven, preach any other gospel unto you than that which we have preached unto you, let him be accursed. As we said before, so say I now again, if any man preach any other gospel unto you than that ye have received, let him be accursed."

Paul had gone into Galatia and preached the Grace of Christ. People were set free, and it was awesome. Soon after he left however, they fell right back under a mixture of law and grace. This is because people known as "judaeizers," or those who sought to preach the Jewish law, came in after Paul and corrupted the purity of the Grace Gospel Paul had preached, and put the people back under a mixed message. They were like bartenders mixing a lethal cocktail.

This still happens today. So often, we get saved by Grace through faith, and we are full of peace and joy, and then soon after we receive Jesus we sit under a "judaeizer" who puts us back under the teaching of, "Now, if you want to stay good with God, you need to do these five things, and avoid these five things." That is mixing law and Grace. If you want people to live in defeat, preach that. If you want people to experience victory, stop mixing that in and preach pure Grace. If you keep mixing it, people will keep dying.

According to this passage, anything other than the unadulterated Gospel of the "Grace of Christ," is "another gospel," which is, "not even a gospel." It fills me with joy that Paul declares that this mixed message of grace and law is no gospel at all! I can testify to the truth of that statement 100 percent in my own life, and maybe you can to. Maybe you're thinking, *"You know what Paul, you're right. The message I have been hearing is actually no Gospel at all! I have been sitting under a mixed message."*

In the Greek, Gospel literally means, "too good to be true news." Now ask yourself, "Is having to depend on my own ability to adhere to religious rules and regulations to stay in good graces with God too good to be true news?" No way! That's no Gospel at all! Amen?

I have no interest in a curse from God, so I earnestly seek to preach pure Jesus. I earnestly seek to preach unadulterated Grace. I have been accused of preaching a license to sin by many fellow pastors in my community and online, and that encourages me! The same accusation came against Paul! I am sure I miss it sometimes, but that is my heart. I only have interest in pleasing my daddy, God, and what pleases Him is to preach the Grace of Christ.

It doesn't please men to preach pure Grace, but it pleases God, and that's the important thing. Paul summarizes this concept beautifully in **verse ten**, *"For do I now persuade men, or God? Or do I seek to please men? For if I yet pleased men, I should not be the servant of Christ."*

You see, Paul is saying that the Gospel of the Grace of Christ is not pleasing to men, but it is pleasing to God. Paul poses the question to the Galatians, "Is my goal to please men? Or is my goal to please God?" Paul declares that if he sought to please men, He wouldn't preach the Grace of Christ, because the Gospel of the Grace of Christ is not pleasing to men! If he wanted to please men, he would preach a mixture... but that is "another gospel," and it is accursed!

No thank you!! Paul was concerned with pleasing God. There comes a moment in our lives where we must ask ourselves, *"What am I seeking? Am I seeking to please God, or am I seeking the praises of man?"* If you truly want to please God, according to scripture we have already covered, you must preach the pure Gospel of the Grace of Christ.

Believing that mixing some law in with Grace is necessary can come from a good place, but a sincere heart motive still does not deduct from the deadliness of this mixture. For instance, you may believe the lie that more rules will actually help people defeat sin. You may really be trying to help people with your rules, but you are ministering from a place of ignorance despite your sincere motive. The truth is the letter of rule following is precisely that which kills people, and awakens and strengthens the desire to sin in their flesh, making it utterly impossible to defeat sin.

I want you to think of someone you love deeply. Now, imagine you unknowingly administer a deadly poison to them. Obviously, you would never want to do this, but you were ignorant of the poison's presence. After they ingest this poison, they will die despite your love for them, will they not? Your love for them, and your desire for them to live is not enough to stop the effect of the deadly poison flowing through their veins. The power of your own ignorance was greater. Now ask yourself, what killed them... the poison, or your ignorance?

Furthermore, their death does not cure your

ignorance. As you stand over their lifeless body, you will still be wondering, "My goodness what killed them? Why did they die?" You are still unaware of the deadliness of your own ignorance. You tried method after method to stop the effect of the poison, but you are really just stabbing in the dark. It never even dawns on you that your ignorance of the presence of a deadly poison is what killed them. This is where people are left when they are taught to try and defeat sin by their own willpower.

God's word teaches that the letter KILLS. To say the letter of legalism doesn't kill is unscriptural. Are we going to agree with God and His Word, and begin teaching unmixed Jesus as He wants, or are we going to stubbornly continue teaching our word, mixing law and Grace to please men, even when it's not what God says?

Think of the person that you loved deeply… if you had been made aware of the presence of the deadly poison, would you not have immediately removed it? Yes, you would! Well, the bible teaches that leading people into relating to God, and judging their own worth and rightstanding before Him by following external laws actually kills them… it is a deadly poison. You have been made aware; now remove the poison! Purify the message and preach pure Jesus! You may have a good heart, but having a good heart does not equal knowledge.

Do you remember my son Harmon and the cabinets? As long as I tell him "thou shalt not open the cabinets," the desire to sin against that command remains strong within him. That command has the power to kill him, because it keeps sin strong in his flesh, and will lead him to act on sinful desires that can have terrible consequences.

23
HARD HEADED

1 Sam 15:23 – *"For rebellion is as the sin of witchcraft, and stubbornness is as iniquity and idolatry. Because you have rejected the word of the LORD, he has also rejected you from being king."*

NOW, THIS CAN be a hard word, but it is a timely one. The context here is the Lord speaking to King Saul through the prophet Samuel. Saul always stubbornly did what He wanted, rather than what God instructed Him. This concept can still be applied today. When we stubbornly teach what we want to teach, when we stubbornly continue to preach from Mt. Sinai rather than Mt. Zion, when we teach the mixture that ministers manipulation and obligation, condemnation, guilt, etc., we are operating under the same stubborn Spirit from which Saul was operating. We are actually being sinful and idolatrous. We know deep down we should be teaching the pure Word of the Lord, who is Jesus Christ, who IS GRACE, yet we stubbornly teach a mixture of Jesus and the law anyway.

This stubbornness is idolatry. We have made an idol and put it before God. This idol is the same as Saul's: our need for the praises of men. God referred to Saul as stubborn because Saul didn't just disregard God's instructions once or twice, but again, and again, and again, and again, expecting different results.

The most sobering part of this is that Saul's kingship over Israel was rejected because of Saul's rejection of the Word of the Lord. You see, God cannot bless a teaching that is in direct opposition to what He has commanded. He can only bless that which He has declared He wants preached. It is stubborn and idolatrous to continue to teach a legalistic, mixed, false Gospel, and God rejects it. He cannot in good conscience lead His precious children to hear such a poisonous message.

So the question becomes, at what point do we change our approach when we've had poor results for so long? Take the pastor's meeting for example… these guys are wondering why churches are dying in our area, and why they are not seeing any results. No one in the meeting ever suggested that we might need to change our approach. They were just complaining about how, "the younger generation doesn't respect the church… these young people have no respect for God. This younger generation is hopeless. They don't care a bit about our traditions."

The young people are rejecting the God religion has presented them. This God is not really God, it is an idol… a perversion of what God is really like, so can we blame them? But, when you share the truth of the Gospel of Grace, and share the God represented in the person of Jesus Christ, it is a God young people want to know! And if you share the true Gospel, God can refill that church with confidence! He can lead his children there knowing they are going to be fed the nourishing bread of life: Jesus Christ!

God declared in dramatic fashion to the men in the meeting that day, "It is time to change your approach!" Let us ask ourselves, when can we shelve our pride, and admit that mixing law and grace is not working for people? How long do you maintain an approach when the results are terrible? Seriously guys! Are we an insane church? I mean, the definition of insanity is to do that same thing over and over expecting different results, right? God is revealing His Grace across the earth, and asking leaders, "Can you humble yourself? Are you willing to change your approach?"

I love to play golf, and when I first began I had a terrible slice! As a right- hander, my shots would curve twenty or thirty yards from left to right! Now, the way to cure this slice and hit the ball straight, was not to stubbornly continue swinging the same way expecting different results. That would make me insane! I needed to change my swing path. I needed to change the way my golf club approached the ball, and therefore change the way the ball flies. Once I changed my club's approach towards the ball, my results changed for the better, and I began to hit the ball straighter.

In the very same way, we cannot stubbornly keep our approach of mixing law and grace the same, and expect our results to improve! This is the question God is posing to leaders everywhere: Are you willing to shelve your pride, and stop pointing people to you, and to themselves, and start pointing people to Jesus? Are you willing to change your approach?

It's time to stop arrogantly teaching self-help behavior modification, and start teaching the unadulterated Gospel of the Grace of God! It's what God wants taught, and I want to teach what God wants taught, and that is His Son! That is Grace! Grace is what brings life and victory; law kills!

24
YOU ARE FREE TO MANIFEST!

NOW, ANOTHER COMMON motivation for mixing legalism and Grace is the incorrect view that born-again, new creations in Christ are still sinful worms that just want to go out and commit all manner of ungodliness; therefore, these sinful monsters need lots of RULES! You think people still need lists of rules because they're untrustworthy and sinful! Again, not scripturally true! If you are born again, you have the very nature of God! <u>Is His nature one that desires sin? NO!</u> Let's read what Paul declares in 2 Cor. 5:17, and learn about the nature we've been given as believers!

> **2 Cor. 5:17** – *"therefore, if any man be in Christ, he is a new creation, old things have passed away, behold, ALL THINGS HAVE BECOME NEW, AND ALL THINGS ARE OF GOD!"*

As a believer, your nature is 100% of God. You DO NOT have a sinful nature. Stop seeing yourself as a sinner struggling to live holy, and begin to see yourself as you actually are: holy and Godly already, and free to be yourself. God declares that you most assuredly have the ability to be an effective representative of Him, and to be holy and spiritual, WITHOUT a list of rules hanging over your head! How? Because it is your nature! Somebody say Amen!

> **Romans 6:14** – *"for sin shall not have dominion (power, authority) over you, for you are not under law, you are under grace."*

You see, for spiritual maturity to manifest in the life of a believer, their new nature must be allowed to come forth, and for our new nature to come forth freedom must be present. Legalism prevents freedom, for it is inherently bondage. Freedom only manifests in an atmosphere of Grace, and maturity only manifests in an atmosphere of freedom. So Grace is prerequisite for freedom, and freedom is prerequisite for spiritual maturity.

Look what the bible says about what happens when the Spirit of the Lord is present. The Spirit of the Lord is not legalism and religion it is the Spirit of Grace. Where the Spirit of the Lord is, there is Grace, and therefore there is Freedom!

> **2 Cor. 3:17** – *"Now the Lord is the Spirit, and where the Spirit of the Lord is, there is freedom."*

25
DEPART FROM ME, SCHOOLMASTER!

MATURITY NEEDS FREEDOM in order to manifest. That's why God is all about freedom. He desires for believers to walk in maturity, and avoid the pitfalls of perpetual sin, which brings destruction in their lives. It all comes back to how much God loves us and is looking out for us. I know this concept can sound difficult, but allow me to illustrate it like this.

This past fall, my wife and I went to visit a nearby house known as the "pumpkin house" around Halloween. This house is so cool… they have thousands of pumpkins with candles inside each pumpkin, with different designs on each pumpkin. It is a real hot spot in our area, and is an absolute blast. You can even get involved and have some ownership in the experience! They allow you to use one of their pumpkin carvers and help them carve more pumpkins to set out. There are families everywhere, and it's just a great time.

My favorite part of the experience is on the left side of the yard. There, is a wall of pumpkins about forty feet wide and fifteen feet tall. There are hundreds of pumpkins on this wall, and they represent an orchestra. Each section of pumpkins is a section of an orchestra. There is a section of pumpkins where each design is a an instrument from the string section, a section where each design is from the horn section, there's a percussion section, and even a section with human faces cut out representing the choir. They have the pumpkins on this wall programmed to light up in time with orchestral music, which is played on a stereo. When the string section is playing on the music, the string section of pumpkins lights up… when the choir is singing, the choir lights up, etc. It makes for an incredibly beautiful and moving experience. Michelle and I were just standing there, holding hands and watching as an orchestral piece played and the pumpkins lit up according to the music, and the Holy Spirit began to speak to me.

He said, "Jake, look how many little kids are here." I scanned the area as He'd instructed, and there were dozens of kids ranging from one or two all the way to thirteen or fourteen. "There's a bunch of kids here!" I said. "You're right, Now, do you see how not even one of those kids is running up to the wall of pumpkins and trying to touch it?" I looked at the wall, and He was right… none of these children, who you would think would be running up to the wall to touch the speakers, or the piles of wires, or the pumpkins themselves, were anywhere close to it. They didn't seem interested in messing with the wall. They were all just keeping their distance enjoying the show.

He said, "Those kids aren't running up to touch the

wall, because this is an atmosphere of grace and freedom, therefore maturity can manifest. There is no presence of law here, therefore maturity is manifesting. If you were to go get a sign that reads, "do not touch the pumpkin wall," and stick it in the ground next to the wall, maturity would no longer be able to exist in the environment, and every kid that can read would be running up to touch those pumpkins."

You see maturity is not defined by an ability to follow rules. Webster's dictionary defines maturity as, "full development." How can you fully develop, if someone is always telling you what to do? Maturity is manifested in the ability to self-govern from the inside out, without someone constantly telling you exactly what to do. This can only happen in an atmosphere of freedom. This is what your new nature is all about. Show me a legalistic church, and I will show you a church full of immature believers that are being kept spiritual babes. Maturity IS NOT defined as an ability to follow rules. Scripture teaches this concept in Galatians 3:24:

> **Galatians 3:24** – *"Wherefore the law was our schoolmaster to bring us unto Christ, that we might be justified by faith."*

When law is being preached, it reveals that the schoolmaster of the law is still leading people, and therefore they are still children. They are being kept spiritual children as long as the law is being preached. Fully developed adults no longer need a schoolmaster, for they have matured out of the need for one. Even more startling, is the fact that the schoolmaster is still leading the pastor, and he himself is still a spiritual child, yet he is leading people. Legalism keeps believers in spiritual kindergarten. Grace leads believers into higher education. Grace allows maturity; law prevents maturity.

You see, the law in and of itself is not unholy, or bad. WHEN THE LAW IS USED FOR ITS TRUE PURPOSE, which is to simply to be a schoolmaster that leads you to Christ, and reveal to you your need for a revelation of Christ, the law is being used LAWFULLY! But a schoolmaster ceases to be needed when you realize what Gal. 3:24 says, that you are not justified by the works of the law, but you are justified by faith in Christ! When you have this revelation, the schoolmaster of the law has served its purpose, and is no longer needed! You see, being great at adhering to religious rules and regulations does not display that you are mature; it displays that you are a well-behaving child.

Think of our children. We teach them, and teach them, and teach them, so that when they finally leave the house, they are able to self-govern. If they cannot self-govern internally, they will be somehow governed externally, whether this external governance comes from you as their parent, the police, their landlord, the water company, the credit card company, whomever. But, as long as they can self-govern, as long as maturity is manifesting from the inside out, there is no need for them to be governed by any external law that tells them what to do (a schoolmaster).

If you must always be in your child's ear telling them exactly what to do, it reveals that they are still a child regardless of their age. Even if they are doing exactly as you say every single time, that does not mean they have matured; it means they are a well-behaving child. When they no longer need you to tell them exactly what to do, then they have matured.

God has given us the ability to self-govern from within, according to our new nature, without a list of rules. He desires freedom for us. We do not need rules to follow for this divine, self-governing ability to come forth; instead we need freedom for it to come forth, just like the children at the pumpkin wall. As soon as I put that sign in the ground that says "don't touch the wall," the maturity of your new nature struggles to come forth, and the sin in your flesh is strengthened. You will regress back to spiritual childhood. Grace breeds spiritual progress; Law breeds spiritual regress.

26
THE TRUTH ABOUT WHAT STRENGTHENS SIN

"BUT I THOUGHT Grace is what strengthens sin." No, law does. This is a life-changing revelation. Check out this verse in 1st Corinthians chapter 15:

1 Cor. 15:56 - *The sting of death is sin, and the strength of sin is THE LAW.*

Notice the Holy Spirit declares through Paul that the strength of sin IS THE LAW, NOT GRACE. Paul lived under the law for a long time, and later in life he received a revelation of Grace, and lived under Grace the rest of his days. So, even naturally speaking, he has authority and credibility to speak regarding what it's like to live under each respective system. He doesn't just know ABOUT what it's like to live under both law and grace, he has actually walked through it… he has a story to tell, a testimony.

Imagine you're in business school. Would you like to

sit under a business professor who is versed in the theory of running a business, but has never actually run one? Or would you rather sit under a business professor who has no formal business degree, but has started 10 businesses, failed 9 times, gotten countless bumps and bruises, learned and persevered, and radically succeeded the 10th time?

If you are like me, you would take professor #2 every time. You could learn how to avoid the pitfalls professor #2 experienced by listening to his testimony couldn't you? You could gain wisdom and apply it without having to learn the hard way as he did. His ceiling could be your floor. You could learn from his failures and from his successes, because He has actually lived it… it is more than theory to him.

You see when Paul lived under the law system; it led to him killing every Christ-professing person he could find in the name of God. He actually had a very sincere desire to please God during this time, but was dramatically deceived, thinking that what the law said was God's heart. Paul even stood by as Stephen was stoned to death. Then, on the road to Damascus in Acts Chapter 9, he actually MET GOD in the person of Jesus Christ! Who is the accurate representation of God? JESUS!! AMEN!

> **John 14:9** - *Jesus said to him, "Have I been with you so long, and yet you have not known Me, Philip? He who has seen Me has seen the Father; so how can you say, 'Show us the Father'?*

All those years of doing exploits in the name of God, and yet Paul did not know God in the least. He thought he knew "about" God because He knew the law. After having an encounter with Jesus however, Paul received a revelation of God's true heart of Grace, and his ministry began to look just like Jesus's, instead of like satan's. He began boldly loving, healing, preaching, teaching, and delivering, instead of hating, persecuting, judging, and killing.

When Paul teaches, he is not just talking about something he knows "about," like professor #1. He is talking about something he was walked through, whether he speaks on law or grace. There was a great deal of wisdom at work in the mind of God (big surprise there!) when God chose Paul to be his main spokesperson in the New Testament. We can learn from Paul and his story like professor #2, and Paul's ceiling can be our floor, or we can stubbornly choose not to learn from him, and continue getting bumps and bruises from learning the hard way. Which do you prefer?

So, as we mentioned above, based on the overwhelming teaching in the body of Christ today, most people think 1 Cor. 15:56 reads like this: "The strength of sin is the preaching of Grace." Hmmmm… It does not say that! It says law strengthens sin, not Grace.

To say that Grace strengthens sin is an utter denial of what scripture teaches. So, if we preach that Grace is a license to sin, we're not preaching God's word, we're preaching someone else's word; an unscriptural opinion at best. You still think people are untrustworthy and need lists of rules.

I want to preach God's word. I want to make Him happy, so I preach Grace. I enjoy seeing people set free, so I preach Grace. I want to weaken and ultimately completely remove sin's hold over people, so I preach Grace. I trust that what God says will help people more than the very best 5 step rule-based system for delivering people my "team" and I could ever come up with.

27
ACCUSATION ERADICATION

MIXING LEGALISM IN with Grace is a pandemic in the church, and as 1 Cor. 15:56 teaches is actually strengthening sin in the lives of people, and making it more difficult for them to live holy and experience victory. It is not helping them. It puts people back under the yoke of legalistic bondage that Paul referred to in Galatians chapter five, right after they've been set free by Jesus and His Grace! Check out Galatians 5:1 and Romans 5:20:

> **Gal. 5:1** – *"Stand fast therefore in the liberty wherewith Christ hath made us free, and be not entangled again with the yoke of bondage (legalism)."*

Rom. 5:20 – *"Moreover the law entered that the sin might abound. But where sin abounded, grace abounded much more"*

So the reality is, Christ has set us free from any legalistic thought process where we are placed under the heavy burden of self-producing life and peace through our performance, and by which we relate to God, yet it is possible to be again entangled in that very yoke of bondage despite this freedom Christ has provided. We do that by allowing ourselves to be put back under rule-based systems for measuring our holiness, our worthiness to receive from God, our qualification for receiving God's promises, maintaining salvation, God's approval, God's love, etc. The yoke of bondage is not only referring to the Ten Commandments written and engraved on stones; the yoke of bondage is a way of believing and relating to God in our MIND. For freedom to manifest in your physical life, it must first take place between your ears. The truth alone doesn't set you free, knowing it does!

When we allow law-based thinking (carnal mindedness) to enter back into our lives, sin abounds as stated in Romans 5:20! Why? Because remember, law strengthens sin. BUT, there is good news, whatever sin we're in, no matter how bad, it can't outreach God's Grace! When sin abounds in our lives, it reveals the presence of legalism. However, when sin abounds, Grace abounds that much more! The supply of God's grace is abundant and inexhaustible! In the Greek, the word used for "abounds" literally means to "hyper-abound, to abound in SUPER-ABUNDANCE!" Just like David, you will always have grace leftover in your satchel. Thank you Jesus!! People bound in sin don't need more law; they need more Grace.

Think of the adulterous woman. Jesus first removed the religious voices of accusation (the hypocritical Pharisees, people from INSIDE the church) from the room so that she could hear Him clearly. He silenced the "misrepresentatives" of God if you will, who had always been misrepresenting the heart of God towards this woman as long as she could remember. However, she did not know they were misrepresenting God. Her understanding was that God was exactly like these angry, bitter, judgmental Pharisees. Maybe that is your understanding too. I pray we can correct that.

The adulterous woman needed a revelation that God's message towards her was different than the one brought by legalistic religion. She needed the revelation that God is not just like religion; He is just like Jesus! This is the revelation that completely changed the direction of my life. It happened in my mind first, and has subsequently let to a change in my actions. Think of Paul… Under the law, Paul's ministry looked like Satan's. Under Grace, Paul's ministry looked like Jesus's.

Now, ask yourself, after Jesus removed those accusing religious voices, did Jesus give the adulterous woman a bunch of rules to follow as a means for her to "go and sin no more?" No, He did not. Why? Because Jesus knows the law strengthens sin, not Grace. Jesus gave her a powerful revelation of His Grace towards her. He declared to her, "I DO NOT condemn you, go and sin no more."

Jesus was so excited to have finally removed the voices of religious accusation from the inner conversation in her mind, and declare the Father's true heart towards her. He rejoiced when He saw relief and thankfulness overwhelm her being!! This lady immediately became an evangelist I almost guarantee! She had reason to shout! She had reason to BE THANKFUL. Jesus understood this truth: thankfulness does not lead to more sin. He gave her reason to be THANKFUL!

28
THANKFULNESS YIELDS FAITHFULNESS, NOT SIN

HE DESIRES THE same for you! Jesus never said sin wouldn't destroy us… it will! It is unwise to live in sin, as its inherent wages are death! Sin is not who we are anymore! We are the righteousness of God in Christ! But, when we sin, when we do slip up and make mistakes, the way out is not more rules; it is God's Grace, and there is always Grace leftover in our satchel. This Grace will produce thankfulness in our hearts, and thankfulness does not produce sin.

For example, when I meditate upon how thankful I am for my wife… when I ponder how faithful she is to me, how unconditionally she loves me, how no matter what she is FOR ME, how whatever I'm going through she is there, thankfulness is born in my heart, and it does not lead me to go cheat on her! Thankfulness leads to faithfulness, not sin.

How crazy would it be to say, "Babe, today I was

thinking about how faithful you are to me, and how unconditionally you love me, and how thankful I am for that, and as I meditated on these things I became so authentically thankful for you, that I felt uncontrollably led to go cheat on you!" Huh? Do you see how backward that thinking is? Grace produces thankfulness, which does not lead to sin.

Now, you do it. Take a few minutes and think of someone who is unwaveringly faithful to you, and all they mean to you. Now, feel peace and thankfulness flood your heart. Is it leading you to go wrong that person? To go hurt them? To go abuse the faithfulness they've shown you? No, thankfulness produces faithfulness, not sin. Look what Paul said in 1 Thessalonians 5:18:

1 Thess. 5:18 – *"be thankful in all circumstances, for this is the WILL OF GOD for you in Christ Jesus."*

Why would it be God's will for us to be thankful? Because it keeps you away from sin! This is why understanding Grace is so important. The more you understand Grace the more thankful you will be. As you stay mindful of what Jesus has done, and how faithful He is to you even when you are unfaithful to Him, that He loves you unconditionally and apart from your religious performance, authentic thankfulness rises in your heart, and begins to lead you away from more sin... just like the adulterous woman. Thankfulness leads to faithfulness.

Furthermore, regarding this license to sin, I want you to realize you never needed a license to sin, nor did you need one to live holy according to rule-based systems. You have always been free to pursue either one before you ever hear anyone preach Grace or Law.

Don't believe me? Let's consider Eve in the garden. Did Eve need an "irresponsible" Grace preacher to come and preach Grace to her before the desire to sin by eating of the tree arose within her? No. She was already "licensed to sin." She was free to sin without anyone preaching Grace to her, by design, as is every other person on earth. So are we then going to call God irresponsible because He designed Eve with the ability to make her own choices? Grace sets people free from sin; it does not set people free to sin. They were already free to sin.

The enemy knows that pure Grace is the very thing that will bring the victory Christians can never achieve through rule following and behavior modification. He is aware of its power to fully and genuinely deliver believers from the bondages of sin, addiction, depression, and all manner of destructive vices. He knows it will set you free, and He does not want that. He wants to keep you bound.

The Word of God teaches that Grace is the very thing that will deliver us from bondage, and teach us to live holy lives. NOT legalistic rule following. Mixing in rule following with Grace keeps believers babes, and prevents spiritual maturity. How can you ever grow up into maturity if someone is always telling you what to do? Even if you always do what they say, it doesn't not mean you're mature, it only means you're a well-behaving child. For true maturity to manifest, freedom must be present.

29
SPIRITUAL LASIC

WE MUST BEGIN to understand, legalism is the devil's right hand man, not God's. Jesus is God's right hand man, and He is full of Grace and Truth, and He ministers love and reconciliation without condemnation (John 1:14-18, John 8). The way Jesus ministers is the accurate representation of God's heart. Check out John 1:18 with me, and I want to show you the definition of the word "seen" in the original language:

> **John 1:18 –** *"No man hath SEEN God at any time; the only begotten Son, which is in the bosom of the Father, he hath declared him"*

The Greek word for "seen" is **horaō**, and it means this: <u>TO DISCERN CLEARLY</u>. Wow!!

So, up until Jesus began His ministry in the earth, no man had EVER discerned God clearly! Amazing! All those hundreds and hundreds of years under the law, and the hundreds and hundreds of years before the law, not a single man had EVER actually discerned God accurately and understood His heart... UNTIL JESUS!!! AMEN!! JOY JOY JOY!! Even the Gentiles who were never under the law, formed their concept of God by observing the Jews, and therefore they too had an incorrect concept of God.

No man had discerned God clearly up until that point, and it was breaking God's heart to see that His precious offspring did not truly know His heart towards them, and how much He loved them! So Jesus comes, and ACCURATELY DECLARES GOD through His earthly ministry! Viewing God through the lens of the law is like trying to see through glasses that have the wrong prescription for you... everything will be distorted and blurry. However, when you put on the glasses of Jesus Christ, and view God through those lenses, you will finally discern God clearly. Jesus Christ is the correct prescription for every person to see God clearly... there is no exception.

It is so powerful that this is declared at the very beginning of Jesus' ministry. The Holy Spirit boldly proclaims to the whole world in this verse: "Look, not a single person has ever perceived God correctly, and God's heart is aching because of it! God wants people to know His unconditional love and grace towards them! This man, Jesus, is about to clear up ALL MISCONCEPTIONS about the heart of God!!" (Paraphrase)

God shouts to every person in the earth through the ministry of Jesus, "LISTEN TO ME! I am JUST LIKE JESUS! If you want to discern Me clearly, view Me through the lens of My Son, not the lens of the law! The law was never designed to reveal My heart towards you, but My SON IS!" (Paraphrase)

Consider where viewing God through the lens of legalism got Paul. Viewing God through the lens of legalism yielded a completely wrong perception of God in Paul's mind. He thought God wanted to kill people. He thought serving God meant carrying out God's murderous will in the earth. Paul was so wrong! His ministry looked like Satan's ministry! His perception of God was so wrong, that Jesus had to visit him in a dramatic encounter on the road to Damascus to correct Paul's tragically incorrect perception of God. Only after this perception correction did Paul's actions change. Many people have died due to the actions of people who had a tragically incorrect perception of God.

Paul himself needed to view God through the lens of Jesus, just as we do, before he finally discerned God clearly. Before Paul could minister in the name of Jesus, and preach the Gospel, he needed to have clear discernment of the heart of God, which only comes through Jesus! This is a radical statement, but if you have not concluded what God is like by viewing Him through the lens of the ministry of Jesus Christ, you should not be ministering in His name.

Look what Hebrews chapter 1 says to cement the foundational point that God is just like Jesus:

> **Hebrews 1:1-3** – *"God, who at various times and in diverse manners spoke in time past unto the fathers by the prophets, Hath in THESE LAST*

> *DAYS SPOKEN TO US BY HIS SON, whom he has appointed heir of all things, by whom also he made the worlds; Who being the brightness of his glory, and the EXPRESS IMAGE OF HIS PERSON, and upholding all things by the word of his power, when he had by himself purged our sins, sat down on the right hand of the Majesty on high;"*

We currently live in "these last days" as Hebrews 1:1 puts it. When I say that I don't say it with an apocalyptic, end times twist. The phrase simply refers to the glorious age in which we are privileged to live: post-Cross, under Grace and the New Covenant. In past times God spoke through prophets, BUT NOW He reveals Himself through the ministry and person of Jesus Christ, and He reveals Himself with perfect accuracy. God was able to reveal glimpses of Himself through the words of prophets, but never His fullness! But the Bible says that Jesus is "THE FULNESS OF THE GODHEAD BODILY!" (Col. 2:9)

We are blessed beyond words to live in a time where we have the ability to discern God clearly through the ministry of Jesus. When we view Him through the lens of Jesus, we can begin to HEAR HIS VOICE LIKE NEVER BEFORE!! This verse describes Jesus as the "express image" of God. Even David, Moses, Abraham, Samuel, you name the Old Testament saint of your choice, DID NOT have the chance to know God like we do, and communicate with Him like we do! When we arrive in Heaven they will ask us what it was like to live in these times!

You will meet Moses in heaven, and you will want to ask him about his red sea experience, and he will undoubtedly interrupt you saying, "We can discuss that much later! I want to know what it was like to have the heart of God perfectly revealed to you through the ministry of Jesus! What was it like to know God so intimately?! What was it like to have Jesus live on the inside of you, and be filled with the Holy Ghost?! What was it like to have a heavenly prayer language? What was it like to be able to command sickness, demons, and all manner of the works of Satan to go in the name of Jesus?!" They will want to hear FROM US what life in this age was like! Prepare to do most of the talking when you arrive in Heaven! We are so blessed!

While God uses Jesus and His Grace to accurately form our concept of His heart towards us if we'll allow Him, ushering us into the freedom of the mind of Christ; the serpent will use law to distort our concept of the Father's heart if we allow him, and usher us into the bondage of thinking with the mind of Adam.

Satan uses legalism to multiply guilt, shame, and condemnation in our lives as believers, keep us fearful of God's anger, and perpetuate the expectation of punishment, which prevents trust in our relationship with God. A Christian bound in legalism will find a way to be punished, even if they have to do it themselves. This breaks God's heart, but makes the devil very happy.

Conversely, God uses GRACE to ELIMINATE guilt, shame, and condemnation from our lives, cast out all fear, and eradicate the expectation of punishment, which creates an atmosphere where you CAN finally TRUST GOD. God's Grace allows trust to foster in our relationship with the Lord by eliminating the fear of punishment.

The adulterous woman had a fear of punishment, which was born from observing religious people her entire life, and deducing what God was like from her observations of these hateful, hypocritical, religious Pharisees. Jesus corrected her wrong perception of God's heart towards her when He proclaimed to her, "I do not condemn you," in the midst of her struggle with sin. Condemnation is never God's voice. Jesus is God's voice.

You should NEVER leave church feeling condemned! Yet, millions and millions of Christians do every week. This is not the Gospel: "Do better! Work harder! Be more pleasing to God! Act holier you sinful worm! Jesus said He would spit you out of His mouth! Get it together! If you make a mistake God will revoke your salvation! You better weep at this altar and re-dedicate (not a real word), or you will burn forever in Hell! This is the Word of the Lord to you today!" WRONG. Condemnation is not God's way of teaching and speaking to you. We mustn't assist the devil by presenting his voice as the voice of God.

Legalism in the church is keeping believers precisely where the enemy wants them: as defenseless babes with no victory, focused on themselves and their own behavior as their Savior instead of focusing on Jesus and His Amazing Grace as their Savior, and unable to hear God clearly because of the earplugs of performance mindedness.

The enemy wants Christians to be a frustrated, unthankful bunch, for he is aware of the power Grace has to produce sin-destroying thankfulness in a believer's life. If he can keep Christians thinking legalistically, he can ensure they will have no reason to be thankful, and therefore frustrate the transforming power of God's Grace in the life of a believer.

The enemy desires to frustrate the victorious power of God's Grace in your life, render you without a personal relationship with Jesus outside of trying to do everything right for Him, and deafen you to God's voice because the voice of your performance is too loud in your ears. He wants you to be hard of hearing to God's voice. The enemy's number one strategy to prevent believers from hearing God clearly for themselves is by inserting the earplugs of performance-mindedness in your ears.

30
THE EARPLUGS of PERFORMANCE MINDEDNESS

> **Gal 2:21** - *"I do not frustrate the grace of God: for if righteousness come by the law, then Christ is dead in vain."*

THE GRACE OF God is the medium through which God speaks. It is the atmosphere that amplifies His voice, whereas legalism is the mute button. When your Christian life is one where you're right-standing before God is based in law following, you will frustrate Grace, and struggle to hear God's voice. You will think the orders and commands you must follow for righteousness are His voice. However, you are actually hearing the voice of the enemy echoing through your performance mindset. He is using your lack of understanding of Grace and the

New Covenant against you, buffeting you, and keeping you in bondage.

Look with me at how powerful this verse is in Isaiah:

Isaiah 5:13 – *"Therefore my people are gone into captivity, BECAUSE THEY HAVE NO KNOWLEDGE: and their honorable men are famished, and their multitude dried up with thirst."*

The less you know about the amazing new covenant, and the amazing grace you live under… the less you know about your son-ship and approval before God… the less you know that God is exactly like Jesus… the less you know that God is always good, and Satan is always bad… the easier it is for the serpent to lead you into captivity. This is why Jesus said KNOWING the truth will set you free. When you begin to gain some knowledge about the truth of God's heart towards you, His love and Grace, you find yourself experiencing deliverance and liberation from religious captivity.

When you begin to taste the freedom on the other side, you will never go back to the yoke of bondage again! You will stay free! But you must learn some things! Ignorance is not your friend when it comes to the Christian life… ignorance is your enemy. If you want to hear God's voice, you must learn about Grace. We are encouraged throughout the New Testament to "Grow in the knowledge of Grace." The more you learn about Grace, the freer you will be, and the easier you will hear the voice of God! To the degree the performance mentality lingers in the way you relate to God, your ears will remain clogged. To the degree the performance mentality is being removed from the way you relate to God, your ears will begin unclogging.

When you have a performance mindset, it does not mean God is not speaking to you... He is... but the atmosphere of legalism is not one where His voice cuts through easily. It is one where the voice of the enemy cuts through easily. The serpent will constantly use your mistakes against you to bring guilt and condemnation. He'll always tell you you're not doing enough. He'll trick you into thinking that because of your mistakes, you deserve punishment. He will even pervert the word of God and beat you over the head with it.

An atmosphere of Grace is needed for God's voice to cut through easily. Until you adopt an unconditional love and grace/effortless son-ship mindset, aka the mind of Christ, you will have trouble hearing Him. This principle is the key to hearing God clearly. You must think like a son, not a slave! You must think in terms of unconditional love and grace, not conditional love and grace based on your performance.

To illustrate how deafening a performance mindset is to hearing what God is actually saying, I want to highlight this passage in Matthew in which the disciples forget the bread:

> **Matthew 16:5-12** - *"And when his disciples were come to the other side, they had forgotten to take bread. Then Jesus said unto them, Take heed and beware of the leaven of the Pharisees and of the*

> *Sadducees. And they reasoned among themselves, saying, It is because we have taken no bread. Which when Jesus perceived, he said unto them, O ye of little faith, why reason ye among yourselves, because ye have brought no bread? Do ye not yet understand, neither remember the five loaves of the five thousand, and how many baskets ye took up? Neither the seven loaves of the four thousand, and how many baskets ye took up? How is it that ye do not understand that I spoke it not to you concerning bread, that ye should beware of the leaven of the Pharisees and of the Sadducees? Then understood they how that he bade them not beware of the leaven of bread, but of the doctrine of the Pharisees and of the Sadducees."*

First of all, notice the disciples had forgotten the bread they were supposed to bring. Making note of that is key to understanding what happens here. Jesus then gives his disciples a loving warning by reminding them to beware of the leaven of the Pharisees and Sadducees. What Jesus is referring to by leaven, as we see further down in the passage, is the incorrect, legalistic, religious teachings of the Pharisees and Sadducees. These teachings are dangerous, as they will quickly spread like leaven, as we see still today in the modern day church. We clearly see here that the will of Jesus Christ is for you to avoid legalistic teaching, not embrace it. Jesus was not giving the disciples a subtle dose of passive aggressive condemnation for forgetting the bread... He was shepherding them... keeping them from drinking from poisonous waters. He is a mighty Savior.

Jesus' heart behind his comment about the leaven was a heart to protect and love his disciples by reminding them not to entertain the legalistic teachings of the Pharisees. However, because the disciples were only mindful of their performance, or in other words only mindful of what they had done wrong in forgetting the bread, they could not hear what Jesus was actually trying to say to them. They thought He was subtly condemning them for forgetting bread. When they heard Jesus's leaven comment, instead of hearing his true heart of love and protection towards them, they began beating themselves up for what they had done wrong in forgetting the bread. They were mindful of their performance; therefore, they could not even understand what Jesus was actually saying. They could not hear His true voice.

Jesus was talking to them, but they could not "hear" Him, metaphorically speaking. Although He was in fact speaking, their spiritual ears were clogged. In other words, because of their performance mindedness, when He spoke they only heard condemnation, when Jesus's heart was NEVER to condemn, but to protect!

The voice of Jesus was filtered through their performance mindset, and what was yielded was a total misunderstanding of what Jesus was saying. This will happen in our lives when we are performance minded. God is speaking to us, but we are filtering it through a performance mindset and misunderstanding Him.

The disciples all suppose together, and reason amongst themselves that Jesus is angry with them because of their mistake. I imagine they began pointing fingers, saying, "Well actually Thomas, YOU were the one responsible for getting the bread, so we're all in the clear, but you're in trouble man. You really messed up. Jesus is gonna whoop you boy!"

Jesus interrupts by saying, *Guys, do you really think I'm worried about bread? Seriously? You think I'm upset because you forgot bread? Don't you remember not long ago when my Father multiplied five loaves of bread and fed five thousand men? Or when He multiplied seven loaves of bread and fed four thousand? Why do you have such little faith? Can you not remember how gloriously God just came through for us just a short time ago? I am not talking about you forgetting bread at all. I AM TELLING YOU TO BEWARE OF THE LEGALISTIC TEACHINGS OF THE RELIGIOUS HYPOCRITES. THESE TEACHINGS ARE DANGEROUS!* (Paraphrase)

The disciples felt relief and peace flood their hearts as they realized that Jesus was not performance minded like they were. Jesus was actually not thinking about their performance at all, ONLY THEY WERE! They assumed Jesus' opinion of them had changed based on the mistake of forgetting bread. They slowly realized that Jesus wasn't beating them up for forgetting bread, He was warning them to stay away from the legalistic doctrine of the Pharisees.

You may need to realize today that Jesus is not performance minded, although you might be. Consider that like the disciples, you may not be hearing His voice because you've been trying to perform for Him, and reasoning from a place of guilt. Even if He speaks in love, you feel inadequate. Even if He comes to edify you, you will still berate yourself. If He comes to encourage, you still feel condemned that you haven't done enough. You must know that Jesus is not judging you that way. He is not thinking about it at all. The question becomes: If He's not thinking about it, WHY ARE YOU??!! Stop! Be free!

All of us, just like the disciples in this passage, tend to think that God is keeping the same record of wrongs on us that we are keeping on ourselves. He's not! We just incorrectly assume He thinks in terms of performance like we tend to, when He doesn't at all. We think when we "forget the bread" so to speak in our lives, His opinion of us plummets. I COME BEARING GOOD NEWS; IT DOES NOT! Just like with the disciples and the bread, He is not thinking about our performance at all. If you can stop being performance minded, you will hear Him better than you ever have.

31
NO RECORD OF WRONGS

LET ME TELL you, when I was growing up, my stepfather was a hard taskmaster. We have a fruitful relationship now, but back then, I hated him! Even though I was a great kid, I was always grounded. With the amount I was grounded, an outsider would think I was surely failing out of school, into drugs, alcohol, vandalism, more serious crimes like candy stealing, etc. But no, I wasn't into any of that. I got good grades, and was on the tennis team for crying out loud... bad kids don't play tennis! ...Well except Andre Agassi... but for the most part... if you liked drugs at my school you played soccer.

In my second year of Bible College, I was assigned to do a ten-minute salvation message in front of about thirty classmates. We were able to pick a pretend audience, and compose our teaching with that audience in mind. I chose an audience of male prison inmates. I thought I could relate to them on the platform of not really having a solid father/son relationship in my life. You see, my dad cheated on my mom and left when I was two and a half, and I didn't have much of a relationship with him growing up. I saw him in the summers, and he would buy me lots of stuff, which I enjoyed of course, but we did not go very deep. I wasn't even aware he cheated until I was eighteen when my sisters told me. I just thought he didn't like my two older sisters and I, and didn't want to live with us.

In addition, my stepfather and I did not have much of a relationship because no trust could ever foster between us, as I was always fearful of him, and always expecting punishment. I could never draw near in that environment, just as we cannot draw near to God when we perceive Him as a hard taskmaster with a heart to punish. My stepdad was a great financial provider, but wasn't very emotionally available or loving. I felt an audience of inmates might be likely to understand the angle of no real fatherly presence in my life, and how God wants to step in and be a good father.

While reading my Bible and preparing for the message, I began to reminisce about growing up. I was flooded with bitterness and anger as I remembered how ridiculous it was that I was always in trouble, when I never did anything wrong. How Shayne (my stepdad) would ground me for a week for accidentally leaving my towel on the bathroom floor. I had friends who were having all kinds of sex, smoking tons of weed, and rolling ecstasy all the time, and they never got grounded! I always thought it was so unfair. I began to get angry at how unloving and mean my stepdad was. In the midst of this angry reflection, I came across a verse in 1 John Chapter 4 that absolutely leapt off the page at me! It was verse eight:

I John 4:8 – *"He who doesn't love, doesn't know God, for GOD IS LOVE."*

As I finished reading that verse, the Holy Spirit spoke to me and said, *"Jake, why are you surprised he treated you like that? He didn't KNOW ME."* I immediately began to weep. To this day it was one of the most powerful revelations I have ever had.

My perspective totally changed in an instant. In that moment, the Holy Spirit delivered me from all anger and bitterness towards him, and I began to see Shayne with intense compassion instead of anger. The tears I wept were no longer for me. I was crying tears of compassion for Shayne. God showed me that Shayne did not really know His heavenly father. Instead of feeling sorry for myself that I never had an enjoyable relationship with a solid father figure, I became overwhelmed with compassion and empathy for Shayne that he did not know the father figure of God at all. I saw that he was parenting me the best he knew how… which was a slightly milder version of the way his father parented him… as a loveless taskmaster. Shane showed love the best he knew how, and he disciplined the best he knew how. His way of showing love was how hard he worked. Shane took us to church every Sunday, and I am so thankful for that, but he did not know God; therefore, he could not love me with God's type of fatherly love, because he himself did not know the Father's love.

Moments later memories of my real dad began flooding back to my mind. I quickly realized that the Holy Spirit was delivering me from all unforgiveness towards him as well. I had been so hurt that he had ditched us, but I had never really talked about it with him… God healed my hurts, and I was able to stop thinking of him as the punk I honestly thought he was up to this point, but thought of him as a man who did not know the father's love for him. A man who was looking to other things to fill the void in his heart that only God could fill.

He had turned away from the church because the image of God he was presented with had been filtered through legalism and religion, rather than the truth, which is that God is just like Jesus. To him, God was an impossible taskmaster, and my dad didn't want anything to do with that God, and like so many other people who've been turned off to the things of God because of religion, he went the other way.

Spending time in the word is so powerful man. I am so passionate about it. God can move so powerfully through His Word, while it's just you and Him! I felt completely renewed after this encounter with my heavenly father. I felt as though I had bathed in a heavenly love waterfall. I needed to continue to prepare for my salvation message, so I continued in the Word. I felt as though I should turn to the love chapter as I had just had a radical encounter with the Father's love.

First Corinthians chapter thirteen, or "the love chapter," as it's known, and verse five leapt off the page. In the NIV, part of the verse simply reads, "Love keeps no record of wrongs." In an instant the Holy Spirit, the incredible teacher that He is, connected the dots for me.

I thought, "Hold on a minute… If God is love, and love keeps no record of wrongs, then who is keeping no record of wrongs??? **GOD IS KEEPING NO RECORD OF WRONGS!"** Praise the Lord! Oh somebody shout! Somebody say amen! I get so emotional and joyful when I think upon how good He is! Praise the mighty name of Jesus!

I eventually came to a point where I felt good about my preparation, and a few days later I went to class to deliver this message. I was a nervous wreck, as I had never preached before in my life. I never even imagined I'd be preaching! I stood up and told a room full of Bible School students pretending to be prison inmates about how God had set me free from unforgiveness toward my two earthly fathers. As I shared the story, people began crying, and the Holy Spirit began touching hearts.

I then told them the truth that although their own conscience was keeping a record of wrongs on them, their families were keeping a record of wrongs on them, their friends, the outside world, their criminal record, etc., all keeping a record of wrongs on them… there was still one person who was not keeping a record of their wrongs, and His name is God! Oh what a radical love the Father loves us with!

My classmates were blessed, but personally I had never felt so charged up or fulfilled as I did after I shared the word that day… it was that moment that I knew I was called into the ministry… I knew in my heart I wanted to spend the rest of my life sharing God's love and Grace through every gift God had given me.

When you see God touch people and bring healing to their hearts, your desire for everyone to experience that same heavenly touch only grows from then on. You simply must tell everyone how much their father loves them regardless of any mistakes they've made.

> **Micah 7:19** – *"You will again have compassion on us; you will tread our sins underfoot and hurl all our iniquities into the SEA OF FORGETFULNESS."*

> **Hebrews 10:17** – *"Their sins and lawless deeds I will remember NO MORE!"*

32
GOD TOO HOLY TO BE AROUND SIN??

SPEAKING OF KEEPING records of wrong, what has happened in the church today is that over time we have come up with our own definition of "holy," and the definition is this: "unable to be around sin." Ignorant of the scriptural fact that Jesus is exactly like God, and He was always around sinners, we say things like, "God can't be around sinners because of his holiness." "We cannot stain the holy garments of God with the sin of those drug addicts." "If only that person would receive Jesus first, and confess every one of their sins, then God could be around them." "Oh, I can't pray with that person. God won't use me because I sinned twice this week. I'm dirty. You pray with them."

Have we ever read about the ministry of Jesus, who is God in the flesh? Jesus spent most of his time with sinners. Not only was Jesus able to be around them, He wanted to be around them. The amazing part is that sinners WANTED to be around Jesus, who was the holiest being in the entire universe. You didn't see sinners running to sit under the religious, hypocritical Pharisees, but you saw them running to sit under Jesus. Funny huh? Sinners did not feel judged or condemned around the holiest person that exists. Perhaps we could benefit from examining if we really know what holy means?

Ask yourself; do you think Jesus was fellowshipping with sinners in their homes pointing out their sin? Condemning them? Judging them unfavorably? I don't think so. He was sharing good news! So in the gospels we see that our religious definition of holy, which says "can't be around sin for sin is too dirty for God," does not hold any water. Let us dig deeper.

The word holy does not mean, "Cannot be around sin. " In fact, it means, "to be full of integrity." With that in mind, let us learn what integrity means. According to Webster's dictionary, integrity means, "a quality or state of being undivided. To be one in word and deed." If God is not divided, that means the Father, Son, and Holy Spirit agree at all times. He is also one in word and deed, or in other words He is absent of hypocrisy. Hypocrisy begins when your words and deeds begin to differ.

Sinners in Jesus's day thoroughly enjoyed His Company for many reasons, but one in particular is that unlike the religious Pharisees, Jesus was not a hypocrite. Jesus meant what He said, and carried out His words with His deeds.

For example, in Luke 4:18, Jesus quotes Isaiah 61:1-2 and proclaims what His ministry is all about. He said this:

> **Luke 4:18-19** – *"The Spirit of the Lord is upon me, because he hath anointed me to preach the*

gospel to the poor; he hath sent me to heal the brokenhearted, to preach deliverance to the captives, and recovering of sight to the blind, to set at liberty them that are bruised, To preach the acceptable year of the Lord."

Because Jesus was holy, or in other words, He was full of integrity, undivided, and one in word and deed, He then spent the next three and a half years making good on this Word that He spoke. He went about doing exactly what He said He would do.

First off, He preached good news to the poor, which in the Jewish culture was incredibly radical and against their traditions. In their culture, the poor did not deserve to hear good news, for they were poor because they had not followed God's law, and therefore were unworthy. For Jesus to preach the same good news to the destitute as He did the affluent was as punk rock as it gets… very anti-establishment! Jesus was anti-religious establishment from the very beginning. Jesus loved the religious PEOPLE the same as all other people, but He did not love their doctrine and teachings, for their doctrines were killing people, and Jesus is the giver of life.

John 10:10 – *"For the thief comes only to steal, kill, and destroy, but I have come that they may HAVE LIFE, AND HAVE IT IN ABUNDANCE."*

Jesus went around healing hearts and bodies, preaching deliverance to people held captive by legalistic doctrine, as well as sickness and demonic possession, He removed the religious veil from people's eyes so that they could see God for who He really is, to discern Him clearly as they never had, and He liberated those that were bruised or wounded of the heart. He did exactly what He said He would do! This is holiness!

The holiness of Jesus is not manifested in an inability to be around sinners. That makes no sense at all. Look at His ministry! The holiness of Jesus is manifested in the oneness between He, the Holy Spirit, and the Father, and the oneness that exists between His words and His deeds.

When we say that holiness is manifested in an inability to be around sin, not only are we fabricating our own false definition, we are actually doing something very dangerous. We are giving ourselves an excuse to stay sequestered within our church walls and avoid the hurting people in the outside world. What we are really saying is that to us, sinlessness is a prerequisite for lovability. That is a tragedy!

We are so programmed to identify people with their sin! For example, when I say the name Lance Armstrong, what do you think of? You think of his use of performance enhancing drugs! The love of God does not identify Lance with his use of performance enhancing drugs. The love of God does not take into account his sin against cycling! If we cannot love people apart from their sin we are as babes.

We are called to love others as God loved us. Ask yourself, how and when did God love you? Was it only after you cleaned up your life? No, it was while you were yet a sinner! So if we are to love others as He loved us, we are to love people in the midst of their sin! In loving them, we stop identifying them with their sin, and identify them as a precious child of God who needs to know the good news of their father's unconditional love for them.

> **Romans 5:8** – *"But God commendeth his love toward us, in that, while we were yet sinners, Christ died for us."*

If you can stop identifying people with their sin, and needing people to be sinless in order to find them loveable, you will be so much happier! The church is not called to identify people with their sin; it is called to love people as Christ loved us. If we can see this, the kingdom of God will spread like wildfire in a world desperate for the father's love.

If you can stop identifying people with their sin, you will find unspeakable depths of joy, and you will actually be relatable to someone who does not know God. You will begin to be in a good mood just like God is all the time. You will begin to be a shining light like never before.

You cannot manifest the agape love of God while still identifying someone with his or her sin. You must see the value past the sin as God does. We must stop identifying people with their dirt, and identify them with the value beneath the dirt.

For example, if I wanted to give you a $100 bill, and this $100 bill happened to be covered in dirt and mud, would you say to me, "I'm sorry, but I cannot take this $100 bill, for it is too dirty"? Absolutely not! I am certain you would take that $100 bill! Why? You would take it because your concern is not with the dirt, but with the value underneath the dirt. I could pay for my meal at a five star restaurant with that muddy $100 bill, and they would not care a bit, but the church cannot seem to see past the dirt.

If a filthy, smelly, drug-addicted, drunk, angry, unpredictable homeless man walked into your church how would you view them? Would you focus on their dirt, and use their dirt as an excuse not to love them with the love that God has shown you? Would their dirt and sin cause them to be unlovable to you? Would you need them to clean up before you could love them? If so, I do not condemn you... I just ask you to reflect on all that God has brought you out of, and how your life is not perfect either, and allow the Holy Spirit to supernaturally give you new eyes with which to see that homeless man. Those new eyes are called the eyes of the love of God. Sinlessness is not a prerequisite for loveability. It wasn't when God sent Jesus for you, and it shouldn't be when you look at other people.

Unbelievers should not be asking, "Man, why can't these Christians love me despite my struggle with this or that sin? I mean, didn't Jesus hang out with sinners? Why aren't these Christians more like Jesus?" (Most know more about Jesus than you think.)

Unbelievers should actually be asking, "What is compelling these Christians to see past all my shortcomings and love me so unconditionally in the middle of my mess? How is it that they seemingly don't even notice how dirty I am? Why are they treating me like I'm so valuable? Man, the love these Christians are showing me feels so good! Who is this God they are representing? I must meet Him!" This is a massive aspect of OUR HOLINESS... the closer we grow to Jesus the less hypocritical we get, and the more attracted sinners are to us.

33
THE POWER OF AGREEING WITH GOD

YOU SEE, GOD is not a hypocrite. He is not a religious Pharisee. He is not legalistic. His word and deed are one. He doesn't say He came for sinners, and then not pursue sinners; only hypocritical Pharisees do that. He came for sinners and He pursues their hearts passionately. He is not an elitist. There is no favoritism with God (Rom. 2:11). He did not come to condemn. He does not keep a record of wrongs. He remembers our sins and lawless deeds no more.

God is far less weirded out by sin than we are. He would have to deny the once for all sin sacrifice of Jesus Christ for Him to make sin an issue between He and man anymore. I did not say we don't make mistakes. I said sin is not an issue between God, and us, and never will be. The Cross completely solved that problem. Will you believe it, and allow your conscience to be washed in the innocent blood of Jesus Christ?!

John 3:17 – *"For God did not send His son into the world to condemn the world; but that the world through him might be saved."*

God is not like the disciples assumed Jesus was, just waiting for them to make a mistake so He could chide them. He does not keep a record of wrongs on you, but as long as you stay under legalistic teaching, you'll always keep a record of wrongs on yourself! You will be tempted to begin believing God is viewing you like you are viewing yourself. You will stop drawing near to him because you are developing an expectation of punishment, and a fear-based way of relating to Him, and fear has torment! This is not God's will.

You see, a performance mindset hardens your heart towards God, and clogs your ear to His voice, not the other way around. When you are overwhelmingly mindful of your performance, rather than your position as a son, you need a RADICAL, POWERFUL removing of the legalistic voices of accusation just like Paul and the adulterous woman did, so you can finally hear God's true voice, which is Jesus.

Why would you be so mindful of your performance, when God is not? Why continue keeping a record of wrongs on yourself, and assuming God's opinion of you has changed based on the wrong you've done, when none of that is actually happening? There is only one true reality, and that is the reality that exists in the mind of God. In His mind you are loved unconditionally.

So, will you agree with this one true reality of God's unconditional love for you? Or, will you choose to continue to live in a false reality where God's opinion of you constantly changes based on your performance? Choose truth. Choose freedom. Choose what's true in God's mind, for that is where you will find peace. God loves you no matter what. You are a child of God who belongs in the father's house. I lovingly urge you to agree with Him!

Do you recall from earlier what the word "confession" means? Remember, it means, "to agree with, or say the same thing as." So, true confession is not listing all the reasons why you're unworthy to dwell in the father's house as a son; that is actually a wrong confession, because you are disagreeing with God. True confession is agreeing with God that you ARE worthy and you ARE a son!

Agreeing with God about how he feels about you is another step to hearing his voice clearly. If you can take this step, and renew your mind to your reality as an unconditionally loved child of God, who belongs in His house, whose sin God remembers no more, you will begin to hear him like you never have before. You will unplug your ears.

Now, although sin is no issue with God any longer, it will still kill you. Sin's inherent wages are death. Sin does not need a helping hand from God to bring destruction in your life… it is plenty potent on its own.

For example, if I choose to go and commit murder, are there not inherent, destructive consequences to such a sinful action? Yes, there are. The "wages" of the murder I have committed are awful. Not only have I ended a precious human life, I will bring unimaginable sorrow upon the friends and family of my victim, change the course of all of their lives, I will bring unimaginable shock and sorrow upon my own family when they learn of my crime, and of course I will have to live with myself afterwards. Is God bringing any of these consequences on me as some sovereign act? No! These consequences are the wages of my action. This is why it's important to learn to live above sin, in victory over it. It has the power to bring mass destruction! And it's not who we are!

I submit to you the way we overcome sinful struggles in our lives is totally by God's Grace, not a mix of His grace and our human ability to follow guidelines by fleshly willpower. God's Grace is needed to transform the lives of believers and bring freedom from sin. I'm not talking about managing sin; I'm talking about being delivered from it.

34

THE FINISHED WORK OF THE CROSS

I WANT TO SHOW you a verse in the book of Titus that will further solidify our argument that Grace is God's means for his precious children to be free from the destructive grip of sin, not a means to stay in sin. Look what Paul says in Titus 2:11-12

> **Titus 2:11-12** – *"For the grace of God that brings salvation has appeared to all men, teaching us that, denying ungodliness and worldly lusts, we should live soberly, righteously, and godly, in this present world"*

AMAZING! The Word of God clearly states here that Grace, the very thing that is perpetually accused of leading people into more sin, is in fact what teaches us to live soberly, righteously, godly, and upright in this present world. Grace actually leads us away from sin! You see, the Greek word for Grace is "charis," and it means, "a DIVINE influence upon the heart." Ask yourself, would an influence that is divine, or in other words is from God, lead you towards sin? Would God influence you towards sin? Does that even make sense? Grace teaches us to live the holy life we couldn't under legalism. However, very few churches teach this. The main reason is because you cannot teach this and control people at the same time.

Rule-following (legalism, law) as a means of attaining and maintaining God's love and approval, holiness, and righteousness, is doomed to fail because that approach is simultaneously strengthening sin in your flesh (1 Cor 15:56, Romans 7), while depending upon the strength (or lack thereof) of that flesh for success in following those rules. Talk about stacking the cards against you!

The devil loves this type of teaching in the church because it kills people, and he comes only to kill, steal, and destroy (John 10:10). God is sick of seeing His children in pain, and He's doing something about it.

> **1 Cor. 15:56-57** – *"The sting of death is sin; and the STRENGTH OF SIN IS THE LAW. But thanks be to God, which giveth us the victory through our Lord Jesus Christ."*

Most Christians think this verse reads like this: "The strength of sin is the preaching of Grace." Remember, 1 Corinthians 15:56 DOES NOT say that Grace strengthens sin; it says THE LAW STRENGTHENS SIN! If we want the power of sin to be destroyed in people's lives, we need to stand against the preaching of law, and stand for the preaching of Grace! We must preach Grace to see people set free.

I think every Pastor would agree that we want people to live soberly, righteously, and upright in this present world, and we want people to be free from sin, right? I hope so… Well, the Word of God clearly declares that GRACE is what teaches people to do just that! NOT a mix of Grace and legalism! One of my favorite quotes is by Andrew Wommack, who is an incredible Bible Teacher, and President of Charis Bible College in Woodland Park, CO. He sums up how we tend to blindly believe a traditional, denominational outlook without ever looking it up in the Word of God ourselves like this: "Sometimes we have to let the Bible get in the way of our denominational theology." Wow.

The law is not designed to reveal the heart of the Father, nor to be a means by which you earn God's approval; it is designed to bring you to the end of yourself, at which point you cry out, "God, I could never do all this right, I need someone to do it for me and as me!" … and that's where Jesus comes in and extends to you the FREE GIFT of righteousness that HE EARNED FOR YOU! The day you cease looking to yourself for right standing with God, and look unto Christ, is the day your life as God meant it to be truly begins. Freedom! Peace! Security! Joy! Amen! Check out how Paul puts it in these two verses in the book of Romans:

Romans: 8:3 – *"For what the law could not do, in that it was weak through the flesh… "*

Once you look away from your fleshly ability to follow laws, which is inherently weak, and unto Christ for your right standing with God, and you finally believe that His sacrifice was enough, you will never go back to the bondage of law-following as a means to earn right standing, for you've tasted freedom. You will finally feel secure, as you understand your salvation is based on Christ, not you.

Romans 10:4 – *"For Christ is the end of the law for righteousness to every one that believeth."*

To deny the sin destroying power of Grace is to exalt denominational, man-created doctrine above the Word of God. You are actually denying the work of Jesus Christ. You are drenched in self-righteousness, because you're actually saying that Jesus didn't finish the job, and you need to add your ability, good deeds, and performance to the equation because His work on the Cross was incomplete.

Can you find peace in the midst of declaring Jesus's work on the Cross is incomplete? Do you think He did a poor job? No! He did a great job, and He Himself declared, "It is FINISHED!" You do not need to add your religious performance to Christ's performance to ensure you stay saved. He authors your salvation, and finishes it.

35
JESUS IS THE AUTHOR, AND THE FINISHER!

NOW, HERE IS what almost every denomination in the body of Christ agrees upon:

Eph. 2:8-9 – *"For by grace you have been saved through faith, and that not of yourselves; it is the gift of God, not of works, lest anyone should boast."*

The overwhelming majority agrees that certainly your initial salvation comes through receiving Jesus as your Savior by Grace, as a free gift, according to Ephesians 2:8-9 written above. Our boasting in regards to salvation is in Christ, and His work, not our works, otherwise we could boast in ourselves and not Him. Amen, this is truth. However, where most denominations begin to disagree, is how you maintain this salvation. Many denominations are teaching Christians, "You better follow these seven rules to the letter to stay saved. If you do not, God will rip your salvation right out of your hands. He's just up there waiting for you to screw up. If you want to avoid hell, from now on no playing cards, no dancing, no shorts, no tattoos, etc. etc. etc."

They teach that your own rule-following ability and willpower are the means by which you stay saved and in the love of God, and measure your holiness. That is not what the Word teaches. In this model your salvation is like the cars the Flintstones drove. Jesus gives you the initial push, but if you want to keep going your little legs better get to work!

This is a fear-based control model. There is no freedom in it. You are always fearful God's going to send you straight to hell if you make a mistake. There is no rest. You're running to the altar to "rededicate" (not even a real word btw) every other week. This is the yoke of bondage!! Christ died to set us free. (Gal. 5:1) This bondage is why so many people stop going to church. Why go somewhere every week just to hear inadequacy, disqualification, condemnation, and guilt? God's design for a church body is to be a place where you can be edified and encouraged, not torn down and condemned.

As a leader, you can certainty control people with this teaching though. You can use this model to make sure people volunteer, show up every week, and the biggest one of all, you can use this model to fear people into consistent giving.

If you tell people they may go to hell if they don't tithe, most people will give out of fear of hell. But, what happens in doing this is you've made giving people's savior, not Christ. If they give, they stay saved, if they don't give, they go to hell; therefore, giving is their savior.

Even worse, is you have robbed people not only of their money, but also of the joy of giving. As people created in the image and likeness of God, part of our design is to enjoy giving. We can see this aspect of our design even in unbelievers all across the world. We see wealthy unbelievers everywhere, who have discovered how much they love giving, and are literally addicted to giving and philanthropy! They do not know it, but they have actually tapped into part of their divine design!

However, the moment we are giving out of fear, manipulation, or obligation, is the moment joy is not a part of our giving. This type of fear-based control in the church is anti-Christ. Christ is the Savior, not the tithe.

This type of teaching hurts people. It is all supposed to be by Jesus's strength in and through you! Initial salvation, AND walking out the Christian life, is BOTH by His strength through Grace. God's design is not salvation by Grace, and walking out your salvation by legalism. Paul puts it like this:

> **Gal. 2:20** - *"I have been crucified with Christ; it is NO LONGER I WHO LIVE, BUT CHRIST LIVES IN ME; and the life which I now live in the flesh I live by faith in the Son of God, who loved me and gave Himself for me."*

It is through understanding Grace, and the finished work of Jesus Christ on your behalf that you will begin to have victory over sin and other struggles in your life. Giving can become fun again, because when you see a ministry that is preaching the true Gospel of Grace and is actually helping people, you will want to give and support the spreading of the message of truth!

The mixing of behavior modification, and rule following into the lives of Christians actually KEEPS THEM BOUND and STRENGTHENS SIN. It teaches them nothing about how to overcome sinful bondage. Grace is needed for that. The Word conclusively teaches that Grace teaches you to live holy, not legalism.

36
UNDERSTANDING HOW GRACE LEADS YOU OUT OF SIN

I WANT TO ILLUSTRATE how Grace is a license to cleaner living, not to more sin, by telling you a story from my past. I want to tell you about something that happened when I was twenty-three. It was a Saturday night, and I was driving my friend Justin and I from one bar to another, and I was pulled over for drinking and driving.

The officer initially pulled me over because I performed a last second maneuver into a left turning lane. The truth was, the intersection I was approaching had two left turning lanes. However, I had not been downtown in a while, and I couldn't remember if the lane I was in was only a straight lane, or was also a turning lane. So, at the last second as I approached the light, I quickly zipped over into the far left turning lane to make sure I was good. The instant I did that, I saw his lights go on and heard the siren. I was immediately terrified.

I had just finished two Maker's Mark (bourbon) and waters. These drinks were about 90% Maker's and 10% water. Back in the day, this was most definitely my drink of choice. I remember how prestigious I felt drinking bourbon while others drank Bud Light… sad, yet hilarious. Now, it had only been maybe ten minutes since I drank them, so I did not yet feel physically drunk, but I knew the alcohol was in my system, and if he administered the Breathalyzer I would certainly blow over the legal limit.

My life began to flash before my eyes. Despair, fear, uncertainty, and defeat overwhelmed my heart. I wondered, "What will I tell my mom? She will be so disappointed." "What about my future? My entire future is derailed now." "How will I get a job after this?" "I'm about to go to jail." "Is this going to be my life? I didn't think I was destined for this type of fate."

My buddy Justin began to coach me through what to do… "Dude, now when He asks you this, say this, and when he wants you to do this, do it this way, etc." I think God placed him there to encourage me, it seemed like he had been through this a time or two! I was actually very thankful!

The officer pulls me out of the car and begins to administer the field sobriety tests. I pass them easily because the effect of the bourbon had not taken yet. Then he did the unthinkable: he pulled out the breathalyzer. I will never forget the words, "Mr. Stringer, I'm going to breathalize you. Are you aware what the legal limit in the state of Kentucky is?"

"Yes officer," I replied.

"It is .08." "Blow into the breathalyzer please Mr. Stringer," he directed me.

At this point I had admitted defeat in my mind. I knew without a doubt I was going to blow over the limit. I knew I was guilty. I knew I was going to get a DUI, and the entire course of my life would be dramatically altered. I knew I was sleeping in jail that night. I knew I would have to watch my mother cry tears of profound disappointment... that one was the one I was most worried about. Disappointing my mom had always been my greatest fear. In fact, I feared disappointing her so much that at that point I had yet to actually do anything with my life. Living in the fear of disappointing someone else will lead to paralysis. This is why so many Christians never step into their purpose. They always think they're disappointing God, or on the brink of disappointing God, so they exist in paralysis, never moving forward into their destiny and calling.

I was so scared of disappointing her; it actually prevented me from discovering my purpose and ambition. I was floundering for fear of disappointing her, instead of living in freedom and pursuing what was in my heart. I thought what I was passionate about would disappoint her. The amazing thing is she never in a million years wanted me to feel like that, but because I never brought it up to her, and I allowed it to fester in my mind, it gained power over me.

If you feel paralyzed for fear your dreams will disappoint God, I declare to you, "Rise up and walk!" "Get up out of that wheelchair!" God never wants you to feel like that. He gave you those dreams… they are actually dreams of His, and He decided you are the PERFECT person to carry them out in the earth! Following those dreams will birth a level of supernatural satisfaction and fulfillment within you like nothing else will, and you will bless the earth!

A few seconds after I blew into the breathalyzer, the results appeared on the screen.

"Mr. Stringer, you blew a .16. That's double the legal limit. How much have you had?"

I nervously began to reply, "Officer, I will be totally honest with you, I do not feel drunk, but I have had two tall Maker's and waters within the last fifteen minutes. I will park my car over there in that parking lot right now and walk. You can park my car over there. Anyone can park it over there, I don't care! Just please don't give me a DUI, I am so sorry!"

After entertaining my desperate appeal, he said, "Stay here, I will be back in a minute." At that point, he walked over to his cruiser and got in. It appeared he was messing with his laptop. I figured he was preparing his DUI paperwork. I was DYING! Every second seemed like an hour. I continued to accept the inevitability of my arrest and DUI charge.

After an excruciating ten minutes or so, he got out of his cruiser and walked back towards me. I was ready to be arrested. When he reached where I was standing, which was in the middle of Limestone St., one of the busiest streets in the entire city, with hundreds of cars driving by, he began to speak. "Mr. Stringer, I have no idea why I am about to do this. I do not believe you're drunk. I want you to get in your car and drive to your destination, and park. Do not drive anymore tonight after that."

"WWWWHHHAAAAAAATTTT??!!" I thought. I was dumbfounded. In a moment of supreme idiocy, I asked, "Are you sure officer?"

He quickly answered, "Yes, and go now or I will change my mind. You are not getting a DUI right now. Go."

I tried to play it cool. Like a basketball player who just had a huge fast break dunk tries to play it cool by acting like his spectacular throw-down was no big deal, I calmly walked back to my car like I wasn't even excited. But inside, I was exploding with excitement, relief, and thankfulness!!

Now, according to the law, I deserved to have my future forever altered in a negative way. According to the law, I needed more rules now to prevent me from getting another DUI. According to the law, I needed to start going to classes to learn how not to drive drunk again. According to the law, I deserved to start paying $800 a month for my car insurance. According to the law, there would be a record of wrongs attached to my name that any employer could view and form a preconceived notion about me based upon it.

What I want you to see is that according to the law, I was guilty. According to the law, I deserved condemnation and punishment. But, despite my guilt according to the law, this officer extended Grace and pardoned me. He extended to me favor that according to the law was UNDESERVED. According to my merit, I deserved punishment, condemnation, and captivity; however, despite my poor merit he released me back into freedom. Despite my actions, and their consequences according to the law, I had been set free. Sounds a little bit like Jesus and the adulterous woman.

Now, according to the accusation against Grace, which says that Grace is a license to sin, after this officer extended this unmerited favor towards me, I would begin abusing it by going out and driving drunk every night after this happened. I would conclude that it would be advantageous for me to take my partying and drunk-driving to an even higher level. After all, the Grace he showed me was a license for more drunk-driving right?

Wrong. That did not happen. What did happen; however, was that such a thankfulness filled my heart for the grace I had been shown, such overwhelming gratitude for the pardon I'd received, that even though according to the law I was guilty and deserving of condemnation, punishment, and captivity, I was extended Grace and granted freedom still, that it allowed me to live a holier life!

You see, I had a revelation of what this officer's Grace delivered me from. This revelation of the grace I'd been shown birthed an immeasurable thankfulness in my heart, and caused me to completely stop driving drunk. I was not about to test the Grace I'd been extended! His grace empowered me, and TAUGHT me not only to stop driving drunk myself, but it also turned me into a "don't drive drunk" evangelist if you will. I would tell anyone that would listen my near DUI story, and plead with them never to drive drunk. The officer's Grace did not empower me to increase my drunk driving. Grace produces thankfulness, which leads you into faithfulness, not more sin.

The other aspect of this experience I would like you to see, is that much like in the instance of Jesus and the adulterous woman, in this officer's hand were two things: the power to punish according to the law, and the power to pardon according to his heart. The law said to punish, but the officer's heart was to pardon; however, in my position, I could not see past my knowledge of Kentucky law, and into this man's heart. My understanding was that Kentucky law and this officer's heart towards me said the same thing. Like the adulterous woman and Jesus, I was fairly certain this officer was going to punish according to the law. Just like Jesus had every right to stone the adulterous woman and punish her according to the written law, this officer had every right to punish me according to the state of Kentucky's written law. But, my understanding of this officer's heart was changed when his actions revealed that his heart towards me was NOT THE SAME AS WHAT WAS WRITTEN IN THE LAW.

You see the law did not reveal God's heart towards the adulterous woman, and nor did the laws of Kentucky reveal this officer's heart towards me. Jesus had a heart to set her free, and this officer had a heart to set me free. As we mentioned earlier, we must understand that the law is not designed to reveal the heart of God; God's actions on the earth through the ministry of Jesus reveal the heart of God. In the very same way, the laws of Kentucky were not designed to reveal this officer's heart, his actions were.

The law simply reveals your inability to earn right standing by your own ability, and that you need a savior, or someone to deliver you and do it for you. In this situation, because I knew that according to Kentucky law I was guilty and in need of deliverance; I needed this officer to be my savior and deliverer. Under Kentucky law, I had forfeited my freedom due to my poor performance. For me to stay free, I needed someone to set me free despite my poor performance, and this officer did that. I am grateful to this day.

This officer's grace towards me was but a type and a shadow of God's Grace towards me, and God's Grace towards you! God's heart is for His children to get a hold of this truth! This begins with church leadership actually having a revelation of Grace so they can teach it. The reality now, is most leaders do not understand the Grace of God and the New Covenant, so they are leading the best they know how. They cannot lead people somewhere they have not been. They have nine toes in the old covenant behavior modification model, and one toe in the New Covenant and the Grace of God.

They will tell you to act a certain way and God will love you. They will tell you to follow these ten steps unto holiness, to delete your social media, to burn your rock albums, etc., etc. This does not fix anything! This is like trying to permanently remove a weed by only cutting it above the surface of the ground. This is legalism at it's finest which actually strengthens a person's desire to sin. These rules they think will help people, will actually lead us into deeper struggle.

37
THE MYSTICAL PULPIT TRUTH SERUM AND CAMP BITTERNESS

IN HONOR OF the trinity, my three main goals in this book were as follows:
1. To help you understand the extravagant, reckless, and unconditional love of God towards you, and receive a revelation of your son-ship, and immeasurable value to your Heavenly Father.
2. To help guide you into a revelation of how to think in terms of Grace, as opposed to law. In other words, to think like a son, not a slave. To be delivered from the mind of Adam, and stop thinking in terms of your performance. To begin thinking like Christ: for it is the only way to think and maintain freedom in every area of your life.
3. For you to gain a practical understanding of how grace is not a license or empowerment unto sin,

but an empowerment unto holiness, and how it is the power of God to give you victory over sin and to live in perpetual freedom in your mind.

I sincerely pray that God speaks to you in mighty, numerous, and profound ways through these pages. I am humbled by the opportunity to write this, and am brought to tears by the thought that I am finishing. As we draw this book to a close, I want to encourage you in two things.

First of all, I encourage you to avoid embracing bitterness towards religion. I encourage you to see religious people as God enabled me to see my stepfather and father… as people who simply could not love me with the love of God because they themselves did not know His love. I believe God will enable you to see people bound in the bondage of legalism and religion with the eyes of Jesus Christ Himself, and He will anoint you as He anointed Jesus to proclaim liberty to the captives.

It is so easy to begin saying, "I can't believe what those people taught me for all those years! I am furious!" … and stay in that place. I am not saying a period of time in which you feel that way will not happen… but what is unhealthy would be for you to set up camp there and permanently lodge at Camp Bitterness. Holding on to that bitterness can be likened to walking behind a crocodile, and grabbing a hold of its tail, and keeping hold of it. That crocodile will bite your arm off! Let go! Unforgiveness and bitterness can kill you!

One of my favorite pastors tells a story of when He was beginning to get a hold of Grace. The more he learned, the angrier he became towards all the people who had preached law to him over the years. He went on a rant about this to his mother, and when he was finished, she simply replied, "Son, didn't you have your own Bible sitting on the nightstand that whole time? Couldn't you have read it yourself?" Wow!

I do not say that to bring condemnation if you have never spent a great deal of time reading your Bible yourself, or to say that God will speak to you in the same manner in which he spoke to this pastor. I use this story to illustrate that God's desire is not for you to set up camp at Camp Bitterness, and live in anger towards law preachers. That will kill you.

Realize they too need a revelation of God's love and grace. Pray for them to have a heart to receive. Pray for them to have a mighty encounter with Jesus like Paul did! And that the entire direction of their life will change just like Paul! Desire for them to experience the same liberation you are experiencing, for living in that place of love for those who may have hurt you, is living in freedom!

Secondly, realize that not everything we hear from a pulpit is truth. That is something I never realized. I believed that if it came from a preacher in a pulpit it was truth. Now I know this is not the case! However, the enemy knows that most people believe that what comes from the pulpit is truth, this is why He uses preachers to preach so many lies… He knows most Christians don't read the bible for themselves, and they will receive the lies being preached as truth.

Andrew Wommack said something that really stuck with me a few years ago regarding sitting under teaching once you've had a revelation of God's Grace and the New Covenant. He said that the Holy Spirit would teach you to quote, "Chew up the hay and spit out the sticks."

This really helped me. You see, we are not called to the ministry of error correction. In other words, going around correcting everyone's theology all the time. However, we are also not called to receive everything that comes from a preacher as truth.

What we are called to do however, is to take what we've heard and weigh it against the ministry of Jesus which is God's true heart. This is rightly dividing the Word. I encourage you to do this as you go forward. It is a healthy practice, and has healthy side effects! It will lead you to spend lots of time with God in His word, which will only bless you!

I want to sincerely thank you for reading this book, and I pray in the mighty name of Jesus that you received something eternal from it. I pray God's mightiest blessings over you and your family, your future, your finances, your job, your calling and your purpose! May you flow downwind with the wind of the Holy Spirit as you go through life! God bless.

Made in the USA
San Bernardino, CA
05 April 2016